Two | AMERICAS

Liberal Education
& the Crisis of
Democracy

Two AMERICAS

Liberal Education & the Crisis of Democracy

Stephen C. Rowe

ANOKA, MINNESOTA 2018

Two Americas: Liberal Education & the Crisis of Democracy
© 2018 Process Century Press

All rights reserved. Except for brief quotations in critical publications and reviews, no part of this book may be reproduced in any manner without prior permission from the publisher.

Process Century Press
RiverHouse LLC
802 River Lane
Anoka, MN 55303

Process Century Press books are published in association with the International Process Network.

Cover design by Susanna Mennicke

Scripture quotations are from Revised Standard Version of the Bible, copyright © 1946, 1952, and 1971 National Council of the Churches of Christ in the United States of America. Used by permission. All rights reserved worldwide.

VOLUME XVI: TOWARD ECOLOGICAL CIVILIZATION SERIES
JEANYNE B. SLETTOM, GENERAL EDITOR

ISBN 978-1-940447-36-0
Printed in the United States of America

CONTENTS

INTRODUCTION

*Tacking Toward a Relational World:
Education as a Scene of Conflict between
Modern and Relational Worldviews*, 1

PART ONE
HIGHER EDUCATION AS MICROCOSM

1

*The Other Conversation: Dialogue,
Meditation, and Service*, 23

2

Standing Up to Managerialism, 37

3

*Rediscovering Liberal Eduation in China:
On the Benefits of Dialogue and Inquiry*, 47

4

The Worldview Problem and Dialogue, 71

5

*The Adulthood We Need: Education and
Developmental Challenge in the U.S.
and China*, 83

6
Ethics, Transformation, and Practice: A Perspective on Liberal Education in the Global Age, 101

7
On Commitment and Civility—and Why the One Requires the Other, 113

PART TWO
BROADER HORIZONS

8
Liberal Education as Cornerstone of Democracy, 121

9
Pragmatism, Possibility, and Human Development, 165

10
Through and Beyond: A Contemporary Soteriology, 181

11
Toward a Relational World from a Western Process Perspective, 203

Acknowledgments, 215

SERIES PREFACE:
TOWARD ECOLOGICAL CIVILIZATION

We live in the ending of an age. But the ending of the modern period differs from the ending of previous periods, such as the classical or the medieval. The amazing achievements of modernity make it possible, even likely, that its end will also be the end of civilization, of many species, or even of the human species. At the same time, we are living in an age of new beginnings that give promise of an ecological civilization. Its emergence is marked by a growing sense of urgency and deepening awareness that the changes must go to the roots of what has led to the current threat of catastrophe.

In June 2015, the 10th Whitehead International Conference was held in Claremont, CA. Called "Seizing an Alternative: Toward an Ecological Civilization," it claimed an organic, relational, integrated, nondual, and processive conceptuality is needed, and that Alfred North Whitehead provides this in a remarkably comprehensive and rigorous way. We proposed that he could be "the philosopher of ecological civilization." With the help of those who have come to an ecological vision in other ways, the conference explored this Whiteheadian alternative, showing how it can provide the shared vision so urgently needed.

The judgment underlying this effort is that contemporary research and scholarship is still enthralled by the 17th century view of nature articulated by Descartes and reinforced by Kant. Without freeing our minds of this objectifying and reductive understanding of the world, we are not likely to direct our actions wisely in response to the crisis to which this tradition has led us. Given the ambitious goal of replacing now dominant patterns of thought with one that would redirect us toward ecological civilization, clearly more is needed than a single conference. Fortunately, a larger platform is developing that includes the conference and looks beyond it. It is named Pando Populus (pandopopulus.com) in honor of the world's largest and oldest organism, an aspen grove.

As a continuation of the conference, and in support of the larger initiative of Pando Populus, we are publishing this series, appropriately named "Toward Ecological Civilization."

-John B. Cobb, Jr.

OTHER BOOKS IN THIS SERIES

An Axiological Process Ethics, Rem B. Edwards
Panentheism and Scientific Naturalism, David Ray Griffin
Organic Marxism, Philip Clayton and Justin Heinzekehr
Theological Reminiscences, John B. Cobb, Jr.
Integrative Process, Margaret Stout and Jeannine M. Love
Replanting Ourselves in Beauty, Jay McDaniel & Patricia Adams Farmer, eds.
For Our Common Home, John B. Cobb, Jr., & Ignacio Castuera, eds.
Whitehead Word Book, John B. Cobb, Jr.
The Vindication of Radical Empiricism, Michel Weber
Intuition in Mathematics and Physics, Ronny Desmet, ed.
Reforming Higher Education in an Era of Ecological Crisis and Growing Digital Insecurity, Chet Bowers
Protecting Our Common, Sacred Home, David Ray Griffin
Educating for an Ecological Civilization, Marcus Ford & Stephen Rowe, eds.
Putting Philosophy to Work, John B. Cobb, Jr. and Wm Andrew Schwartz, eds.

INTRODUCTION

TACKING TOWARD A RELATIONAL WORLD

Education as Scene of Conflict between Modern and Relational Worldviews

I

IT'S LIKE THERE'S NO MIDDLE ANYMORE. It's as if the binary logic of modernity has grown to such massive proportions that it has shaded out all possibilities between terms of polarized opposition. Everything is either this or that, one ideology or the other, with us or against us, 0 or 1. Missing is the middle, the open space where conversation, deliberation, and inquiry take place, and along with these practices—arguably the most crucial for civilizing education,[1] democracy, and healthy relationship—the accompanying experiences of possibility, discovery, emergent truth, growth, recreation. We are talking about the paradoxically open ground of civilized life, that space in the absence of which we are condemned to isolation and mere exchange, to the descent of personhood into the sad and boring condition of mechanism, of positions forever fixed in opposition.

And then there is the slippery underside of late modernity, the tendency for its order to become proteanness (Hannah Arendt[2]), its definiteness to become liquidity (Zygmunt Bauman[3]), and its obsession with objective rationality to roll over into the situation where "lying is the message" (Masha Gessen[4]). On the one hand, we have opposing, absolutized ideological positions. On the other hand, and lurking under these absolutized positions, we have the relativism of all positions. This relativization reveals itself 1) in the market terms of privatization and commodification, or 2) in the "whatever" lifestyles of people who have lost the capacity to think, who navigate through life unable to perceive any value beyond immediate self-interest and banal interpretations.[5] Our social and political situation seems to be more and more one of weird combinations of polarity and flux.

Sailing close to the wind, tacking tight up against the risk of merely exemplifying the problem of opposition that, once posed, could admit of no escape, I suggest that there is indeed an underlying distinction by which the many other terms of opposition (between ideologies as well as between the ideological and the relativistic) can be understood and addressed.

There are actually *two* Americas at this point in history, two very different underlying worldviews in/as America, which is to say, two very different deep understandings or paradigms as to the nature of reality, meaning, and value.[6] One is the modern, Cartesian, natural rights view of separated individuals defined by their right to pursue and protect material well-being in a world structured and governed by the laws of Newtonian science and the competition of free market capitalism, along with the assumptions of both unlimited natural resources and the privileged status of humans (which is inevitably to say *some* humans). The second worldview is both relational and process-oriented, focused on thriving as a condition of harmonious relation into which flows the mysterious and ever-renewing source of vitality on which life itself depends. The relational worldview has deep roots in Western history, as it does in nonWestern traditions as well, with Socrates and Jesus being the most obvious points of Western origin. And it has always been the underdog, since it is deeply threatening to traditional, scientific, and capitalist absolutisms on one side, and post-traditional relativism on the other. Another way to say this is that the relational worldview presents perhaps the highest order of developmental challenge for human beings: the challenge to move beyond both absolutism and relativism into a worldview that contains elements of both, within a vision of mutuality, as the locus of ongoing creativity on this planet.

Turning to the conflict between these two worldviews in both American and global contexts, it is as though we live in a time of smashing, subducting tectonic plates, with one riding up and over, grinding the other under, taking its place in the sun, and quite literally condemning the formerly external plate to the underworld of life on this planet. I want to focus on the smashing and grinding between the Late-Modern worldview (including the neopatrimonialism Francis Fukuyama identifies as the emerging counterpoint to modernity), and emerging relational worldviews.[7] My concern in both education and society has been the conflict between two very different versions of America and the world that are locked in the drama of our era. One embodies the modern worldview, briefly described above. This version threatens all traditional cultures and increasingly draws the rage of a new kind of anti-imperialism that "turn[s] terror into an end in itself."[8] The other version is expressive of a distinctly postmodern culture that, among its other basic characteristics, calls for reappropriation of both some traditional and some modern values, especially those associated with cultivation of the fully adult human being within an environment that is both global and pluralistic.[9] Obviously, the latter is more supportive of democracy.

In this book, I focus on the conflict between the two Americas just described as it is manifest in contemporary higher education, which serves as both a lightning rod for the conflict and a prism through which we can see the essential dynamics of the larger culture in especially clear and effective ways. For higher education still stands, though in some considerable question today, as the gateway to adult life in a larger society that continues to assume an intimate connection between national well-being and educational opportunity. As such, the conflict of worldviews within higher education can help us to understand the underlying tension in American culture—and perhaps in global culture as well, including the latter's surge in ambivalence toward modernity,[10] modernization, and America. Higher education itself can be an educative microcosm.

The active hope I recommend is that there is still time to address the unhealthy drama associated with disjunction between two fundamentally different worldviews in higher education and society today, time to study and learn from the contemporary condition of both university and society, time to navigate through it, into a new era of dynamic stability and adventure. I should say at the outset that I am aware of the improbability of this hope, and that I speak with an optimism that is consciously chosen, preferring the risk of being proven a fool to that of living as a cynic.

II

So, let us zoom in on higher education, and the sense in which it can be a helpful microcosm of the conflicts associated with a larger cultural shift:

In fairly recent times, through historical consciousness, tenuous interdependence, liberationist and ecological awareness, the radical limitations and injustices of the dominant Western, Cartesian worldview are being unmasked. Arising in 17th-century Europe, this worldview expressed itself in isolated and competitive individualism, mechanistic and materialist science, blindness to the chauvinism of the cultural and religious groups through which it originated and progressed, and obsession with being free from everything that had gone before. By the 20th century there emerged a worldwide awareness of the addictive and constrictive effects of the Cartesian worldview and the beginnings of rebellion against it—as in T. S. Eliot's "The Waste Land" (1922), or Alan Ginsberg's "Howl" (1955). As though in response to the arising of this consciousness, by the end of the 20th century Cartesianism began to respond by tightening its grip in an addictive monoculture of consumerism, invasive management, and commitment to high-speed technology that outruns human capacity at every turn. Along with the tightening came terror, as the indiscriminate urge to destroy everything modern, including those who have enjoyed its benefits; with terror itself as a final expression of modernity and its dangerous preference for the blank slate.

Meanwhile, in the midst of these aggressive and reactive forms of late modernism, another worldview, one that is global with an American variation, has been coming to the fore: the relational worldview. It has deep roots also, appearing from time to time in the West: 1) in various forms of Greek and Judeo-Christian culture; 2) in the Renaissance; 3) in early modern democratic movements; 4) in the American tradition of governance through voluntary associations and the independent sector;[11] 5) in some forms of activism and feminism; 6) in process philosophy; 7) in new science via Einstein, Bohr, and others; and 8) in recent social scientific understandings of human development and maturity.[12] As people like Amartya Sen, Sor-hoon Tan, and Tu Weiming have pointed out, the relational worldview needs to be understood as an orientation with "global roots," such that Western (re)discoveries of the relational dimension should not be taken as unique or exceptional.[13] What is common among the various manifestations of this worldview is the awareness that there can be no one, final formulation of what is ultimate in life. Human beings grow into our integrity through relationships with each other and the interaction of our differing views, and that relationships honoring this understanding, and the sense of possibility associated with it, are the locus of discovery, meaning, and even the deepest source of the energy we need in order to live well.[14]

American higher education, like other institutions, has contained elements of both of these worldviews for a long time, and cohabitation—even occasional synergy— between them has been more or less possible. In recent times, however, conflict has come to the surface, especially as it has become clear that the modern, Cartesian lifeway is not only unsustainable, but also impossibly cramped as a home for the human spirit. A series of factors, including the arising awareness of which I speak, has led Cartesianism in the university to tighten and become less tolerant of its relational nemesis: diminishing support for education as a public good, privatization and corporatization of both education and society in general, careerism, and commodification of the curriculum and the degree. I refer to the combination of these factors and their resulting mode of leadership in higher education as "managerialism," a mode that wants standardization, quantity, and assured outcomes. These values are so directly antithetical to the relational vision of meaning, as distinct from measurement, that one wonders: do historical eras, as they end, inevitably throw up their underlying characteristics in high relief, and become aggressive?[15]

Somewhat surprisingly, the relational worldview has at the same time begun, as it had in the earlier Progressive Era and in the experimental education movement of the mid-60s to 70s, to present a compelling alternative vision of education and well-being. Reaching for a more complete description of this worldview — one that is challenging to describe because it is essentially both transformational and pluralistic, in recognition of the ineffability of that which is ultimate in life — I point to five interdependent components of the relational worldview as it is manifest in higher education today.

1. *Integrative/Developmental.* Education must be concerned with more than just ingestion and regurgitation of knowledge, specialized information, and skills that can be installed in one part or another of the person. Rather, education must also be integrative of the whole person and involve transformation within a broadly understood context of developmental movement 1) from absolutistic/ideological insistence on there being one right answer for all questions,

through 2) an individualistic/relativistic stage where success within the increasingly unrestrained competitiveness of market capitalism is the only criterion of well-being that can be generalized, and finally 3) into pluralism, where capacity for democracy, dialogue, and hermeneutical awareness are recognized as necessary for the collaborative and just problem solving of fully adult human beings.

2. *Otherness as opportunity.* Pluralism/democracy/dialogue is identified as both the end *and the means* of education. This is to say that encounter with the Other who is and remains different (neither homogenized and reduced to the same, nor subjugated) is understood as the most vital environment for healthy growth as well as effective problem-solving.

3. *Paradox of service.* That particular kind of encounter in which opportunity for mutual well-being is most intense has been characterized as "service learning." Often misunderstood or misplaced as a college requirement that no one can really explain, "service" indicates the essential element of caring or compassion, as well as the point in our development where we become capable of convening and sustaining the relationship of service—or some would say "mutuality," "reciprocity," or "justice"—in all dimensions of our lives. The paradoxical discovery that our "enlightened" self-interest is best served in caring for others helps us break out of the self-centered and ultimately self-defeating individualism of modernity.

4. *Contemplative epistemology.* Western culture has been driven by the tension between idealistic rationalism and materialistic empiricism, but it turns out there is another way of knowing, one through which we can be more fully present in our genuineness. Through the findings of contemporary neuroscience, as well as reappropriation of mystical traditions left behind in the rush of modernity, we learn "mindfulness,"

as a way of both being ourselves and being responsible—in a way of adulthood and human attentiveness that is more developed than that envisioned by our modern ancestors in their thrall to the mechanical.

5. *Inquiry orientation.* The life we commonly share with others is manifest as problems/questions/issues. *Inquiry* indicates the democratic method through which we address these for the betterment of the world, through considering more and less adequate answers to local manifestations of the eternal question: What should we do? Inquiry within a civic life is understood as the locus not only of the deepest challenges for our own growth (as "we," not just "me"), but also as the inevitable context for the nurture and education of our children and the human exercise of stewardship of life on this planet (in religious terms, assuming the position of co-creators).

Through the partial enactment of these interdependent—not sequential—components in recent decades, higher education, as a major American institution, has made considerable gains in terms of multiculturalism, inclusion, fulfillment of what we have come to refer to as second and third generation human rights, and some movement toward ecological civilization. As evidence of this movement, we can identify a nexus of vitality at the intersection of some of the most influential associations informing higher education today.

On better days, many American universities can indeed be celebrated as representing a "moral and spiritual framework" that is a real alternative to modernity and close to an ideal global community of mutual thriving. Meanwhile, students have benefitted from a curriculum that is less oriented to rote learning and training, and more toward cultivation of the expanded sense of adulthood the world so urgently needs. Of course, students have also experienced the imperatives of consumer satisfaction and the consequences of their colleges' wish to have a good "retention rate," along with pedagogies that are too often ready to congratulate most any kind of self-expression.

This is to say that the more promising developments have occurred simultaneously, strange as it may seem, with American higher education allowing itself to be colonized by the same narrow-minded and materialistic logic of order and control that Western culture exported to the rest of the world in the colonial period. It is as though we have learned nothing from a century of the postmodernism and cultural critique we teach in classes. Again, there is much to be learned from the microcosmic aspect of the American university.

Finally, and not to deny the power of these constraints, I suggest we not underestimate the power of the components discussed above to help American higher education overcome its captivity to the modern value-free orientation in which it has been locked since the 19th century. Unlocking through the introduction of values such as these could enable the university to claim a kind of agency we so urgently need, and hence be able to exercise informed leadership in critical issues such as those of justice and the environment. For a good example of the former, see Sheryl Petty's volume *Social Justice, Inner Work & Contemplative Practice.*[16] On the latter, consider John B. Cobb, Jr.'s recent statement:

> When the future habitability of the planet is in question, one would expect that the enormous research capacities of universities would give attention to how self-destruction can be avoided. For nearly half a century thoughtful people have been aware that we need an economic theory that pays attention to the consequences of our actions for the natural world. We need to have an agriculture that regenerates the soil rather than eroding it. We need to build cities that do not separate people great distances from their work and thus require ever more energy-costly transportation. Serious proposals about how to deal with these matters have been available but ignored by the university research establishment: ecological economics (Daly), perennial polycultures (Jackson),

and arcologies (Soleri). No comparably promising responses have been produced by the research establishment. This total failure greatly increases the dangers we face today.[17]

III

I should identify myself as someone who is neither the modern, detached, objective observer, nor the postmodern critical theorist who only wants to deconstruct.

I am a professor who has been, along with my institution, deeply (even religiously, one might say) committed to "liberal education in a public context," understanding this vocation as, in the words of Marilynne Robinson, "America's Best Idea."[18] I have worked for over forty years and in several capacities—always including teaching—at Grand Valley State University, which has grown very rapidly to become a Carnegie-rated "masters large" public university. We have been diligent in our efforts at inclusion and the education of non-elite citizens, and we have been strenuously committed to and grounded in "liberal education" from the very beginning. While the meaning of this term has varied in some interesting ways over the years, we have been remarkably consistent in being student-centered, undergraduate-oriented, and focused on a substantial and required General Education Program for all undergraduates (including those in professional programs). And our General Education Program is one defined not only by subject matter or "distribution," but also by pedagogy—with discussion-sized classes, tenure-track professors (rather than graduate students, adjuncts, and other "contingent" faculty), primary texts, and writing papers rather than taking machine-gradable tests.[19] Our pedagogy has been aimed not just at information, but transformation—guided by the vision of an expanded form of adulthood which is emerging in our time.

We have always had our challenges, especially those associated with the high cost of this kind of education on a state budget. But as we have grown we have been fortunate to attract professors for whom teaching is their primary practice, with research following as the way in which the fully functioning teacher engages the same transformative discipline they share with their students, enacting a real commitment to the educated citizen as the root of American vitality. Thus there has been a general sense that the strength of the university arises largely from the integrity of our relationship with students, in the culture of a learning community. It is, of course, extremely difficult to measure this crucial quality of synergetic mutuality, though easy enough to chase it away in the process of trying, especially in an era of accountability to "stakeholders" who do not necessarily understand what we are doing.

For me, like many of my colleagues, the classroom has been compelling. Despite having to read a very large number of student papers on any given weekend, there's been an energy associated with knowing our students well, both in person and in writing (again, with a student-faculty ratio very different from that of elite colleges), such that many of us have wound up being more productive in our own scholarship than colleagues at more elite institutions. So I have not regretted my choice to participate in what a good number of my early colleagues, coming to this bold and somewhat improbable new university saw as a logical extension of 1960s activism, which sought, as Martin Luther King, Jr., said, to "make real the promise of democracy,"[20] reflecting John Stuart Mill's insistence that a society that protects the "liberty of action" necessary to a democracy is only possible among "human beings in the maturity of their faculties."[21]

In recent years, however, the levels of challenge and constraint have reached new highs, and they seem to have arisen from within the university as much as from without. It has appeared that something new is going on. But I have doubted my perceptions and been so busy, so caught up in the multitasking lifeway that keeps so many of us—in the university and out—away from any real thinking, that I have not had time to confirm or critique my perceptions through conversation with friends and colleagues (in the midst of ever more emails and text messages, no time/space for anything like democratic deliberation.)

Maybe the sense of professors being deprofessionalized reflects a failure on my part to understand the imperatives of the large-scale organizations universities have become. Maybe the standardized Syllabus of Record and data-driven assessment schemes really are inevitable expressions of an unfortunate separation between professors who teach and an ever-expanding army of administrators who possess much demographic information but have little to no contact with students as persons in their primary learning environments. Maybe the disrespect for the instructional function of the university that emanates from a fair number of administrators and support staff is part of the cost of institutional success. Maybe they, in turn—those administrators—are too much under pressure from accrediting, legislative, and other agencies external to the actual educational work of the university. Perhaps they are too far removed from the joys and sorrows of the day-to-day educational encounter that is the heartbeat of university life.

But no, something new and something deep is indeed going on, something that is in no way unique to my own university. Some critical threshold has been passed. In fact, my university has been enough of an exception to what is going on in U.S. higher education (and in other national systems, as far as I can tell) that it has allowed me and others to keep our heads above the tide of change washing over us, and to keep some perspective on what it all means for the actual—and often over-assessed but little understood—education of students. From this perspective, it is clear that American higher education is teetering on a fundamental threshold on the far side of which "liberal education"—or even "civilizing education"—could be commodified to become a mere slogan, indicating, at best, a commitment to consumer satisfaction. Mind you, this is not entirely a bad thing, but it is not at all the thing we had intended, or the thing we want as our primary indicator. And my root discipline of social ethics, founded on the attempt to facilitate the partnership of thought and action in the direction of a better world, has required me to address the condition of American higher education as reflective of the underlying conflict in American culture. This is the conflict between the modern Cartesian worldview, in what must be its last days, and an emerging postmodern vision of relationality, which is in need of help with both articulation and embodiment.

IV

The essays that follow all arise out of the broader understanding described above. Because of the more circular, less hierarchical, and conversational nature of the relational worldview they advocate, the order is not strictly sequential, as in the linear unfolding of propositional logic, traditional systematic philosophy, or religious doctrine. The relational worldview is best presented as *tackings,* movements upwind, to the degree that is possible at any given time, at a sufficient angle to the wind to keep the sails full and the boat moving windward, rather than simply being driven downwind.[22] This mode of travel is very different from that of the speedboat, which could take us directly upwind to our destination. The speedboat is fast, but it operates on the delivery model, which is analogous to rote learning in education. Speedboats discount the significance of the journey—plus the ride can be uncomfortably choppy. The tacking process, on the other hand, does make progress toward the goal—whether it be civilizing or readiness for employment—but it also values what happens along the way and leaves space for the integration human beings need. Tacking avoids the here-to-there mentality that regards all journeys in terms of destinations and all destinations as matters of either tourism or business.

Therefore I conclude this introduction with very brief summaries of the essays that follow, to help the reader decide what they may want to read and in what order.

PART I: HIGHER EDUCATION AS MICROCOSM

The Other Conversation. This essay presents three crucial developmental dimensions beyond rote learning: 1) dialogue as reflection, reflexivity, the ability to evaluate one's own position as well as those of others with respect to meaning and value, and be open to emergent truth through encounter with the other; 2) mindfulness as the awareness of both self and world associated with what is sometimes called "contemplative knowing," coming from the inside through rather than the outside to, as distinct from traditional rational and empiricist ways of knowing; and 3) service as that compassionate engagement with the world which is paradoxically the best thing one can do for one's self.

Standing Up to Managerialism. A brief description of "managerialism" as the aggressive form of late-modernity that seeks order and control through the mechanization of strategic planning and assessment, the worldview it represents, and the fragile alternative of the relational worldview, which is also at work in the contemporary American university.

Rediscovering Liberal Education in China: On the Benefits of Dialogue and Inquiry. A report on pre-Xi Jinping conversations with Chinese colleagues about their efforts to reform their education system and appropriate elements of Western liberal education, or in Chinese, usually 素质教育或通才教育 or "broad" education, often understood as education oriented to critical thinking, creativity, and innovation. Progress of that conversation identified cultivating mature humanity as the shared fundamental aspiration of "liberal education," and understood in these times as the value of the classics of both Chinese and Western culture in this light. This essay also contains an argument for the necessity of "comparative general education," or the global dialogue of our era as the healthy environment for revitalization of higher education, including reappropriation of traditional wisdom.

The Worldview Problem and Dialogue. A description of the new worldview that is emerging in our time, and its close linkage to the developmental vision in which "dialogue" is understood as one of the signal capacities of the mature human being.

The Adulthood We Need: Education and Developmental Challenge in the U.S. and China. An examination of the capacities-based approach to education, which has largely superseded distressed discussion about what should constitute "the canon," or the appropriate subject matter of education. Examined also is the vision of healthy human development, which underlies the movement to focus on capacities, as well as their interdependence within the relational paradigm.

Ethics, Transformation, and Practice. More focus on pedagogy, now through necessary components of a civilizing education.

On Commitment and Civility. On the paradoxical co-presence of these two qualities in the mature person; on how the authentic definiteness of commitment requires openness to the other as a possible source of the truth and discovery, arising from mutual problem-solving, and ongoing identificantion and refinement of one's commitment.

PART II: BROADER HORIZONS

Liberal Education as Cornerstone of Democracy. Democracy is a form of governance that requires an active and informed citizenry who share material resources sufficiently to enable all members of society to participate. This means citizens also need skills beyond those that will enable them to earn a living. Widespread availability of liberal education is an essential component of any society that seeks to sustain democratic institutions.

Pragmatism, Possibility, and Human Development. A 21st-century presentation of pragmatism as a perspective compatible with and supportive of the relational worldview.

Through and Beyond: A Contemporary Soteriology. A tracking of the same developmental movement that has been fairly well-mapped in its psychological dimensions as "life span development," now as a spiritual, cultural, and essentially educational journey.

Toward a Relational World. Several "glimpses" through the inherently pluralistic relational worldview at the dynamics of encounter with both self and other, through religion, civic life, and human development.

My hope is that this collection of essays, written from the perspective of vigorous teaching in the tradition of liberal education, can help us be more alert to the choices that are being made — for better or for worse — in the turmoil of higher education and American culture today. For rather suddenly we have sailed into waters where there is little valuing of higher education, or much else, it seems, except in economic terms, where confidence and persuasive articulation among educators is disturbingly low, and where the seductive appeal of purely quantitative methods of planning and assessment runs very high. The conjunction of these factors underlines the sense in which that characteristic phrase of our time, "the perfect storm," is no mere cliché. We could lose a major boat.

Again as a social ethicist, but, above all, as a citizen committed to civilizing education, I think that among our various problems we suffer from a poverty of interpretation and of conversation about what is going on and what we really value. We need a conversation that can replace the endless complaining, accommodating, ideological dispute, and cynical withdrawal, one that can actually help us wake up to effective action. Such a conversation can help us make choices that affirm the potential of our students and our children — and society generally. It is this kind of affirmation that is so much at risk today, which is to say, that is being forsaken in favor of training what the Nazi architect Albert Spear called "technological barbarians." So I offer these essays in the spirit of that conversation, and in the conviction that, in a very real way, open conversation itself is the answer we seek, and the relational America we need.

ENDNOTES

1   Since *Educating for Ecological Civilization* (Anoka: Process Century Press, 2016), I have stopped using the term "liberal education" as the

most complete and developmentally significant form of education, and begun using the term "civilizing education." This helps correct the view of liberal education as an exclusively Western, Greek practice. "Civilizing education" also corrects the implied negative aim of "liberal education" as liberation *from,* with insufficient emphasis on the positive aims of education. See (with co-editor, Marcus Ford), "Introduction: Education as Civilization," 1–13, and Jiahong Chen and Peimin Ni, "Cultivation of Humanity Through Stretching Liberal Education," 145–65.

2   Hannah Arendt, "What is Authority," in *Between Past and Future: Six Exercises in Political Thought* (New York: Meridian, 1963), 95.

3   Zygmund Bauman, *Liquid Modernity* (Cambridge: Polity Press, 2000).

4   Masha Gessen, "The Putin Paradigm," http://www.nybooks.com/daily/2016/12/13/putin-paradigm-how-trump-will-rule/.

5   Elizabeth Minnich, *The Evil of Banality: On the Life and Death Importance of Thinking* (Lanham: Rowman and Littlefield, 2017).

6   One might argue that there have always been two Americas, that this duality is as essential to what the world's first consciously and decidedly modern society is about, as it is to modernity itself—ending in our day in a weird and dangerous combination of polarity and flux. My best recommendation on the ambiguities of modernity is Stephen Toulmin, *Cosmopolis: The Hidden Agenda of Modernity* (Chicago: University of Chicago Press, 1990).

7   Francis Fukuyama, *Political Order and Political Decay: From the Industrial Revolution to the Globalization of Democracy* (New York: Farrar, Straus & Giroux, 2014).

8   See Kenan Malik, "Radical Islam, Nihilist Rage," in *New York Times,* January 4, 2015: "What Jihadism does not possess is the moral and philosophical framework that guided [previous] anti-imperialist movements. Shorn of that framework, Jihadists have turned terror into an end in itself." Another powerful statement of the kind of terror which develops in the absence of a coherent moral and philosophical alternative to modernity is described by Nietzsche as "willing the void rather than being void of will." See Friedrich Nietzsche, *The Genealogy of Morals*, in Francis Golffing,

trans., ed., *The Birth of Tragedy and the Genealogy of Morals* (Garden City: Doubleday Anchor, 1956), 299.

9   I pursue this conflict and its implications in broader terms in my *Overcoming America/America Overcoming: Can We Survive Modernity?* (Lanham: Lexington Books, 2012). Here I am especially careful to caution against simple anti-modernism, pointing to such "modern" values as material and civic security, individual self-determinism, and pluralistic—if not democratic—community as among those modern values we would not want to reject.

10 See Peter L. Berger and Samuel P. Huntington, eds., *Many Globalizations: Cultural Diversity in the Contemporary World* (New York: Oxford University Press, 2002).

11 On the presence of a "relational liberal" subtradition which was shaded out by Cartesianism, see my *Leaving and Returning: On America's Contribution to a World Ethic* (Lewisberg: Bucknell University Press, 1989), and *Overcoming America/America Overcoming*. On the presence of this subtradition in the broader history of the West, see Alfred North Whitehead, *Adventures of Ideas* (New York: Free Press, 1933).

12 On the latter, see Robert Kegan, *In Over Our Heads: The Mental Demands of Modern Life* (Cambridge: Harvard, 1994).

13 Amartya Sen, "Democracy and its Global Roots," in *The New Republic,* October 2003; Sor-hoon Tan, *Confucian Democracy: A Deweyan Reconstruction* (Albany, NY: SUNY Press 2004); Tu Weiming, in *The Global Significance of Concrete Humanity* (New Delhi: Center for Studies in Civilizations, 2010).

14 A major expression of the relational worldview, and an attempt to find ways to provide alternatives to the modern, Cartesian worldview, occurred in the form of a conference at Pomona College, June 4-7, 2015: "Seizing an Alternative: Toward an Ecological Civilization." (PandoPopulus.com/conference/). On the higher education section of this conference, see Ford and Rowe, eds., *Educating for an Ecological Civilization: Interdisciplinary, Experiential, and Relational Learning* (Anoka, MN: Process Century Press, 2017).

15 For detail on managerialism, see my "Standing Up to Managerialism," in *Liberal Education,* Summer 2014. It is important to

note, in relation to the recent history of higher education, that the "Seizing an Alternative" conference follows the 2007 Fetzer Institute-sponsored conference, "Uncovering the Heart of Higher Education: Integrative Learning for Compassionate Action in an Interconnected World." See Parker Palmer and Arthur Zajonc, *The Heart of Higher Education: A Call to Renewal* (San Francisco: Jossey-Bass, 2010).

16 Sheryl Petty, ed., *Social Justice, Inner Work & Contemplative Practice* (www.contemplativemind.org) for The Initiative for Contemplation, Equity & Action (ICEA), 2017).

17 From a recent, informal lecture given by John B. Cobb, Jr., "The Role of Education and the Degradation of Nature," Loyola Marymount University, Nov 1, 2017. See also Cobb's *Spiritual Bankruptcy: A Prophetic Call to Action* (Nashville: Abington Press, 2010), especially Ch. 6, "Secularist Education, 89–106.

18 Marilynne Robinson, "Save Our Public Universities: In Defense of America's Best Idea," in *Harper's* Vol 332, No. 1990, March 2016, 29–37.

19 I tell the story of my own university as an attempt to embody liberal education in my as yet unpublished essay "Seeking the Mind of Liberal Education: The Case of Grand Valley State University."

20 Martin Luther King, Jr., "Letter from a Birmingham Jail" in *Why We Can't Wait* (New York: New American Library, 1963), 86.

21 John Stuart Mill, *On Liberty*, 1.9 (Indianapolis: Bobbs-Merrill, 1956), 13.

22 Emily Dickenson's image of "Tell all the Truth but tell it slant—" is very attractive here, and related to the contemplative epistemology mentioned earlier. See Allisa Alexander, ed., *The Norton Anthology of Poetry* (New York; W. W. Norton, 1975) 870–71.

Part ONE

Higher Education as Microcosm

1

THE OTHER CONVERSATION

Dialogue, Meditation, and Service

Education is the point at which we decide whether we love the world enough to assume responsibility for it. -Hannah Arendt[1]

I

UNDER ALL THE CHATTER ABOUT EMPLOYABILITY, student debt, market-oriented reform, and whether we really need anything like liberal education, there is another conversation going on in American higher education today. It arises from an expanded vision of adulthood and well-being, focused on capacities and practices through which a new adult state of being and acting in the world can be cultivated, including the (re)discovery of contemplative ways of knowing. This second conversation generates much less noise than the first, and, especially because of its developmental nature, it is more difficult to understand.[2] It could well turn out, however, to be the more powerful and hence more consequential of the two. It could turn out that the second conversation is the medium through which the ancient and ineffable ideal of liberal education is coming to fresh embodiment in our time.

I write in the service of that second conversation and, more specifically, in an effort to help clear up the frequently confusing cluster of terms that appear, often together and sometimes interchangeably, in its discourse: high impact learning, community-based learning, mindfulness, critical thinking, service learning, diversity, attentiveness, contemplation, transformation, reflection, meditation, otherness, reflexivity, inclusivity, social action/justice, integration, multiculturalism, and dialogue. Part of the problem is that most of these terms, though not newly coined, are quite new to the conversation about higher education. At the same time, it could be argued that at least some of them reach down to the deep roots of the traditional Western vision of full human development (perhaps nonWestern visions as well). So these terms share not only energetic association with importance and possibility, but also considerable confusion as to what they really mean and how they are related.

As a result, many of us who participate in the second conversation stumble along in an atmosphere of both enthusiastic acknowledgment and danger that the discussion can be degraded to high-sounding language that is either empty, cliché, or — worse yet — deflected into the service of purposes that are far from those of their origin. This is the condition I want to address, by proposing a simple distinction between three interdependent developmental practices through which these terms can be understood and advanced, within the rich but frequently muddled second discourse of education in our time. I propose dialogue, meditation, and service as primary practices corresponding to the developmental levels through which a new paradigm of education and adulthood is emerging.

Confusion arises in large part because all of these terms are reflective of the sensibilities and intuitions of a genuinely new era. They are glimmers of a way of knowing and relating; ways of learning that are deeper than can be envisioned through the modern dichotomous thinking of either idealism or empiricism, value or fact, objectivity or subjectivity. They are deeper than the bundle of unexamined assumptions that constitutes the flooring of the contemporary research and employment-oriented university;[3] and beyond the indiscriminate critique, deconstruction, and reductionism of most "critical theory" and "postmodernism."[4] Glimmers of a new way arise from the sense that there is something more than either absolute/ideological Truth or relativistic personal preference, something all people can be in touch with and live well by, all the while maintaining and enhancing their distinctiveness. It is precisely the *absence* of sensibilities and intuitions of this sort—of something deeper and different from what the prevailing modern mindset and its institutionalization in our educational systems could apprehend—that led the great social ethicist, James Luther Adams, to conclude that absence of "disciplines of the inner life" was a primary reason for the failure of 1960s activism.[5] It could be that the second conversation reflects no more than academia's passing interest in new terminology—buzzwords that academia is all too quick to embrace without critical examination and then abandon for the next fad. But it could also be that now, nearly fifty years after Adam's remark, we are addressing this root issue through the emergence of the three practices I have identified, and that they together—in the midst of and through the tumult that surrounds them—are moving us into a distinctly post-postmodern world, a world where cultivation of "the inner life" becomes virtually indistinguishable from a new relationship with the world.

At the center of this emergence, the rediscovery of the contemplative way of knowing is perhaps the most radical and necessary for our era. It indicates a way of knowing quite distinct from the rationalism and empiricism that dominated Western culture throughout the traditional period, knowing either top-down from abstract first principles, or bottom-up from the collected data of experience. Either way, within this paradigm, knowing is of an objective order of reality external to the "inner lives" of persons as anything other than thinking machines. The contemplative, by contrast, represents a way of knowing that comes from within, from the inside through rather than from the outside to. It requires renunciation of objectification and intellectualization as prerequisites of knowing, and it accomplishes this through cultivation of the inner silence, attentiveness, or the "not knowing" of which Socrates spoke (before his wisdom was eclipsed by the rationalism of Plato, or, rather, by what became the orthodox *reading* of Plato.)[6] It also requires a kind of relationship with the world, other, and self that is beyond the dichotomy between self-sacrifice and competitiveness.

In our time, the contemplative is being rediscovered and its efficacy certified not only by the testimony of mystics, but also by the contemporary catholicity of science.[7] This rediscovery has enormous implications for both personal and communal well-being. It holds the promise of liberation from the colonization of human consciousness by the Cartesian worldview that has dominated Western — and thereby global — culture since the 17th century. This worldview is characterized by the distinctly modern values that are now recognized as so problematic and/or unsustainable for their addictive hold on the human race. These values include isolated individualism, competitiveness creeping into every dimension of life, materialism, and an evermore "value free" and mechanistic system of technology, economy, and education.

For higher education, the great rediscovery revolves around the dynamics of cultivating the inner life in a way that does not involve retreat from political life, but its enhancement. The possibility opens up that education can be something much more than either acquisition of knowledge and/or technical skill, or, alternatively, withdrawal from the world into isolated self.[8] Now it becomes possible to think in terms of activation of capacities comprising a maturity or form of adulthood that, though not entirely new to the cultural and religious history of the human race, becomes a democratized possibility for all people — and perhaps, as well, a necessity for our survival. This is an adulthood in which we have greater self-transcendence through calm awareness of our responses in life, of that which triggers our defenses and aggressiveness, and thus a greater capacity to live beyond those impulses in a centered, creative presence.

On the contemporary landscape of higher education, in the spaces between the poles of modern dichotomous (or Cartesian) thinking, we see the three practices of dialogue, meditation, and service being reawakened and engaged. The rather long list of terms cited earlier in this essay can then be organized and understood in terms of these practices or capacities, which are also associated with developmental stages. In this world, the nautilus shell is a more adequate image than the upward sloping straight line.

These capacities and practices, understood specifically in relation to adult development as the ultimate aim of education (and hence also in some respects as "levels"), are richly described by Robert Kegan. He describes those who are longing for "the fifth order of consciousness," which is becoming possible in part (and somewhat ironically) due to the simple extension of life expectancy afforded by modernity. He writes of longing

> for the recognition of our multiple selves, for the capacity to see conflict as a signal of our [over-identification] with a single system, for the sense of our relationships and connections as prior to and constitutive of the individual self, and for an identification with the transformative process of our being rather than the formative products of our becoming.[9]

II

The first capacity/practice is *dialogue*. This level entails moving beyond the dichotomy of, on the one hand, rote learning and propositional logic, and on the other, assertions of unexamined, unrefined personal preference (the latter being the typical liability of what used to be called progressive, alternative, or experimental education), and opening up the capacity for understanding and reflection on a variety of positions, including one's own, on any given issue. It also involves the ability to be responsive to emergent truth as an essential quality of full and healthy relationships, democracy, and mature thinking. It indicates the ability to thrive in a pluralistic environment where encounter with the "other" is welcomed as opportunity rather than suffered as threat, where "diversity," "inclusiveness," and "multiculturalism" are not mere concessions to the fragile interdependence of the 21st century, but positive values to be nurtured and celebrated. Is this not precisely what Socrates had in mind when he advocated "the examined life," the life of examining both self and others on the most important questions in life "as the very best thing" a person could do?[10] The life he advocated is associated with contemporary uses of "reflexivity" and "critical thinking." It is something much greater than the ability to recognize bad logic and/or psychological manipulation; something more like the exercise of the discernment indicated by such traditional terms as *phronesis* (Greek for "practical judgment") or *upaya* (Sanskrit for "skillful means").

However, echoing the theme of aspiration by Kegan above, Daniel Yankelovich and others note that the expanded capacity for dialogue and a new adulthood, one which is more alert, more deeply responsive, and less ego-driven by aggressive/defensive impulses, is not one that most Americans are capable of at this time, though it is one that is being pushed by many efforts at educational reform.[11]

The second capacity/practice is *meditation*. Moving beyond the dichotomy between theoretical and applied (or "productive") knowledge, here we are talking about engaging in a practice that allows us to have access to the deeper sources of knowing and action, and to cultivate a way of being we have come to associate with "mindfulness," or the full presence of "attentiveness." The world and its varied traditions contain many such contemplative practices, with remarkable similarities and differences. Essentially, they involve the paradox of clearing and calming one's mind and thinking nothing, with the aid of a very specific object of mental focus (or "mantra," such as one's breath.) The resulting state of calm focus then leads to the Socratic "not knowing" (*aporia*), which becomes an opening to a more profound level of awareness (more like the *source* of knowing than the objects of knowledge flowing from that source). These practices are often simple, though never easy. And, while there can be many arguments about the true nature of this practice, no such practice can be fruitful apart from the actual experience of entering into it and then introducing refinements as they are discovered along the path of actual engagement. On that path—and from the perspective of others who witness the transformation of those who are walking it—meditation is extremely persuasive in terms of stress reduction, emotional stability, concentration, compassion, and effective relationships at all levels. There develops a very significant change in the overall quality of presence following directly from its engagement. The persuasiveness of meditation is aided by the recent findings of neuroscience, as well as continuing reappropriations of those mystical traditions that had been dismissed in the tempest of modernity.[12]

Third is *service*. Moving beyond the modern dichotomy between self-interest and self-sacrifice, genuine "service learning"—sometimes called community-based learning, social action, or even global learning—extends regard for the other, which is necessary for dialogue, to a more active will to engage with the life of that other. This willingness to engage the other includes the senses in which that other's life is shared with our own, in a broader ecology that is synonymous with affirmation and covenant with life itself as a normative principle.[13]

The practice of service is centered on a point well understood by the great traditions: that the end of meditation is to stop "meditating" as an extraordinary activity separated and protected from the messiness of ordinary life. In other words, the ideal end of meditation is that it becomes our ordinary way of being. The end is to be meditating all the time, to "return" to caring or compassionate relationships with both other and self. Martin Luther King, Jr. was eloquent on this utterly crucial point, one that had been excluded from the modern mindset:

> From time immemorial men [sic] have lived by the principle that 'self-preservation is the first law of life.' But this is a false assumption. I would say that other-preservation is the first law of life. It is the first law of life precisely because we cannot preserve self without being concerned about preserving other selves. The universe is so structured that things go awry if men [sic] are not diligent in their cultivation of the other-regarding dimension.[14]

It is this same quality of a life-giving relationship that is indicated by the classical Western love of the world (*amor mundi*, per the Hannah Arendt quote at the beginning of this essay), or the Confucian "human-hearted persons establish others if they want to establish themselves."[15] Active caring and creative citizenship become both marks of true enlightenment and sophisticated forms of practice. Service comes to be associated with the wholeness of the person, and hence the integrative and transformational dimensions of education, through which everything we have studied and become is brought to the essential moment of our authentic being in the world and its ongoing refinement.

As is clear in the great traditions, genuine meditative practices issue not only in a calm and alert state of mindfulness, but also in an actively compassionate presence in the world. Indeed, the great traditions provide perhaps the best explanation for the paradoxical relationship between mysticism and social action, or—to use the language of contemporary higher education—engagement, or civic involvement. To cite an old Zen saying: Easy to meditate in the monastery, more difficult in the home, most difficult in the world. In other words, the fullness of meditation or enlightenment is not detached purity but the developed capacity to sustain that way of being in the midst of effective presence in ordinary life, exemplified by figures such as Gandhi, Mother Teresa, Martin Luther King, Jr., Thich Nhat Hanh, and Sheri

Liao. More so, enlightenment is found not only in the ordinary life of the monk doing mundane chores such as cleaning the toilet, but also in the effort to liberate others from suffering in its many forms. In Mahayana Buddhism, for example, the high religious figure, the Bodhisattva, is not the one who drifts off in mystical detachment, but rather the one who *returns* to help others, the one whose embodiment is that of *karuna* (compassion) rather than *karma* (the accumulated consequence of past action driven by fear, ignorance, desire). Note the parallel, for example, with Christianity and its "commandment" that we "love thy neighbor as thy self." The paradox of service learning and its prominence in higher education today is that, in teaching students the value of serving others, ultimately we help students discover where life is rich and vital, the dynamics of "thriving" or "flourishing" (two other key words in our time), which enhance their own lives. When we approach service with awareness of its full significance, we help students (and ourselves) discover and embody the identity between service and dialogue, as well as between meditation and service—in a way of being that is constituted by a complex and endlessly unique pulsing of interdependence.

III

All this—these three practices and capacities—is simple enough to understand intellectually (and even enjoyable to think about), though by no means easy to grapple with existentially because of the *developmental* aspect, which means that we are stretched beyond our ordinary and inherited ways of thinking, speaking, and acting. For this same reason, this way of being is also vulnerable, as reflected in Alfred North Whitehead's statement that "[g]reat ideas enter into reality with evil associates and with disgusting alliances. But the greatness remains, nerving the race in its slow ascent."[16] Contemporary programs in American higher education that link meditation and mindfulness to service learning and the justice dimension, through civic engagement and social activism, often by way of vague "interdisciplinarity," are therefore especially vulnerable to confusion, incomplete understanding, cliché, and those "disgusting alliances" to which Whitehead refers. Cultivation of the critical linkage is dependent on teacher selection and training that was rare in the past (or unacknowledged, or even at odds with the process of acquiring a Ph.D., let alone becoming an administrator/manager). In the same way, authentic fostering of the values of inclusion, diversity, and otherness require sensibilities and awareness that were also rare among faculty, and certainly no more deliverable in a quick faculty training program (or the artificial order of a "strategic plan") than they are reducible to managerial protocol. Finding the faculty and support staff (and students) we need, in order to embody the new vision of culture and education that is struggling to emerge, is probably our most profound challenge. How, in the environment of contemporary higher education, can we identify and then support those who are capable, providing them with the development they need, let alone then place them in positions where they can do real good?

Fortunately, some educational leaders have emerged, such as the feminist and philosopher of education Elizabeth Minnich, who are able to

> make a case for an overlap of thoughtfulness and mindfulness as arts and ways of being for which we can purposefully educate, not as in some traditions to win release from the world but, entirely on the contrary, to accept our responsibilities as conscious beings affected by and affecting the worlds around us with every breath, action, and word.[17]

The work of Parker Palmer and his Center for Courage and Renewal should be especially noted in this regard as well.[18]

On this same question as to whom we can look to for resources and support, there are two other sources I would point to as reliable in terms of insight and practice. The first is the Association for Contemplative Mind in Higher Education (ACMHE).[19] This organization arises from the emergence of the new interdisciplinary field of cognitive science and a rapidly emerging complementarity between modern scientific rationality and the practical wisdom of the contemplative traditions. Its mission is "to educate active citizens who will support a more just and compassionate society." This is accomplished through "recovery and development of the contemplative dimension of teaching, learning and knowing," leading to "an ethics of genuine compassion."[20]

The second agency that exemplifies the crucial healthy relationship between meditation and service is the YESplus Program and its "Art of Living" course.[21] Arising out of the Hindu tradition, and drawing on the resources of contemporary cognitive science, YES stands for "Yoga, Empowerment, and Service." It is distinctly responsive to the linkage between meditation and service, working to a point of merging the two activities into a fully transformed and integrated way of being. Examples of how YESplus has been joined with local programs and initiatives can be seen at Cornell, Stanford, and Brown.

So with this chapter I am proposing simple clarification of some of the more sensitive terminology of our time, and at least hinting at their unification in an emerging, post postmodern worldview and vision of the educated and fully formed adult. And, as an essential quality of that worldview, I am seeking to illuminate a developmental pathway that some of our more exemplary students travel in the direction of becoming the sort of adults we so urgently need.

However, clarification must be followed immediately by a caution, especially when developmental movement is involved. As we practice the teaching art through which we guide students, we must be careful not to let "levels" and "stages" fall into yet another simple linearity, a risk that runs high in an era that is also characterized by the urge to quantify and standardize. Against these late, more or less desperate assertions of the modern, mechanistic worldview, we need to insist, with all the creativity and persuasiveness we can muster, that the practice of cultivating the new adulthood is *an art*. It is an art that can benefit greatly from science and technique in many forms, especially today through the discoveries of neuroscience. But, insofar as it is humans and not machines we are cultivating, art must be the embracing and integrating quality of education. In what might be the most profound challenge to the technological era, we can only reclaim and develop our humanity through the inherently unpredictable dynamics of human relationship. And today we have the advantage of ever greater sophistication as to what this means.

ENDNOTES

1   Hannah Arendt, "The Crisis in Education," in *Between Past and Future: Six Exercises in Political Thought* (New York: Meridian, 1963), 196.

2   Stephen Rowe, "The Adulthood We Need: Education and Developmental Challenge in the U.S. and China," in *Reflect, Connect, Engage: Liberal Education at GVSU,* Judy Whipps, ed. (Acton: Xanedu Press, 2013); "Liberal Education as Adulthood: A View from U.S.-China Dialogue," *Philosophical Analysis* (《哲学分析》) 23.1 (2014): 145–51; in English, *Journal of General Education* 64.1 (2015): 65–73.

3   John Cobb, "The Anti-Intellectualism of the American University," *Soundings* 98.38 (2015): 218–32.

4   Rowe, *Overcoming America / America Overcoming* (Lanham: Lexington Books, 2012).

5   James Luther Adams, "The Changing Reputation of Human Nature," in *Voluntary Associations: Socio-cultural Analysis and Theological Interpretation,* ed. J. Ronald Engel (Chicago: Exposition Press), 31.

6   Jacob Needleman, *The Heart of Philosophy* (New York: Alfred A. Knopf, 1982); Alison Jagger, "Love and Emotion in Feminist Epistemology," *Inquiry* 32.2 (1989): 151–76; Pierre Hadot, *Philosophy as a Way of Life: Spiritual Exercises from Socrates to Foucault* (Malden: Blackwell Publishing, 1995).

7   Francisco J. Varela, Evan Thompson, and Eleanor Rosch, *The Embodied Mind: Cognitive Science and Human Experience* (Cambridge:

MIT Press, 1993).

8   Arthur Zajonc, "Contemplative Pedagogy: A Quiet Revolution in Higher Education," *New Dimensions for Teaching and Learning* 134 (Summer 2013): 83–94; Parker Palmer, Arthur Zajonc, and Megan Scribner, *The Heart of Higher Education: A Call to Renewal* (San Francisco: Jossey Bass, 2010).

9   Robert Kegan, *In Over Our Heads: The Mental Demands of Modern Life* (Cambridge: Harvard University Press, 1994), 351.

10 Plato, "Apology" 38a, in *The Collected Dialogues of Plato,* ed. Edith Hamilton and Huntington Cairns (New York: Parthenon Books, 1985), 23.

11 Daniel Yankelovich, *The Magic of Dialogue: Transforming Conflict into Cooperation* (New York: Simon & Schuster, 1999), 17.

12 Daniel P. Barbezat and Mirabai Bush, *Contemplative Practices in Higher Education* (San Francisco: Jossey Bass, 2014).

13 J. Ronald Engel, "What Covenant Sustains Us?" in *Existence with Ecological Integrity: Science, Economics, and Law,* Laura Westra, Klaus Bosselmann, and Richard Westra, eds. (London: Earthscan, 2008), 277–92.

14 Martin Luther King, Jr. *Where Do We Go From Here: Chaos or Community?* (Boston: Beacon Press, 1967), 180.

15 Confucius, *The Analects of Confucius.* Roger T. Ames and Henry Rosemont, Jr., trans. (New York: Ballantine, 1998), 110.

16 Alfred North Whitehead, *Adventures of Ideas* (Cambridge: Cambridge University Press, 1933), 19.

17 Elizabeth Minnich, "The Evil of Banality: Arendt Revisited," *Arts and Humanities in Higher Education,* 13.1–2 (2014): 162.

18 Parker Palmer, *The Courage to Teach* (Hoboken, NJ: John Wiley and Sons, 1998); Palmer, Zajonc, and Scribner, *The Heart of Higher Education: A Call to Renewal;* For more information, see: www.couragerenewal.org/.

19 The Association for Contemplative Mind in Higher Education at www.couragerenewal.org/.

20 "Mission" and "Vision" statements, The Association for Con-

templative Mind in Higher Education, accessed 2 February 2016, http://www.contemplativemind.org/programs/acmhe/.

21 YESplus Program and its "Art of Living" course found at www.YESplus.org/.

2

STANDING UP TO MANAGERIALISM[1]

"MANAGERIALISM" REPRESENTS A RELATIVELY NEW ORIENTATION to college and university administration, one that arises from the coincidence of three distinct features of the contemporary landscape: market rationality, nihilism, and the modern wish for a new beginning. Here I want to offer a simple clarification as to the nature of this phenomenon and take note of its affinity for programs of strategic planning and assessment. My suggestion is that managerialism is a major factor in struggles over the shape and substance of education today, and one that is not friendly to education as the cultivation of human beings that we so urgently need. But, on the positive side, I suggest that an alternative is available and gradually emerging in our educational communities and practices.

THE THREE FEATURES

Market rationality represents the advance of scientific rationality and commodification into areas that had previously been governed by professional judgment and the art of teaching (and also, in the complexity of our situation, by unacceptable values associated with race, gender, class, etc.). With this feature we have what some refer to as the "corporatization" of the university, indicating admiration and adoption of what are taken to be the standards of business in a free market economy. The influence of this feature is greatly enhanced and lubricated by the incredible advances in computer technology of recent decades, combined with economic insecurity, reduced confidence in education, and a generalized tendency to see little possibility between extremes of capitalism and communism. And because market rationality focuses attention on cost-benefit analysis and what is measurable, rather than on more challenging questions of meaning and relationship, it is a powerful temptation in an era characterized by great uncertainty and huge changes that are not well understood. Market rationality offers at least the illusion of order and control.

Nihilism refers to the tacit conclusion that all relationships and transactions in the world can—and should—be understood not only in terms of money, but more generally in terms of interest and power. Ideals, principles, and commitments are not to be trusted; they should be seen as the projection of someone's interest. This late modern understanding, sometimes implying that "the common good" and "the invisible hand" were myths all along, means that alliances are grounded in nothing more than temporary alignments of interest, resulting in constant wariness and suspicion, even among those with whom one is allied for the moment. This feature is frequently expressed 1) in aggressive "deconstruction" of those who attempt to maintain "higher" values, and 2) in competitive social construction wherein one claims possession of the dominant interpretation of any given situation, especially in the war of all against all that has become so explicit in late modern society, and, ironically, the very condition from which early modernity sought escape.

The third feature, the wish for a new beginning, indicates that quintessentially modern desire to be free from everything that has gone before, in order to wipe the slate clean and start over. Here, unwritten understandings, history, and local wisdom count for nothing,² or worse, are scorned as projections of someone's previous domination.

Managerialism is the mode of administration that emerges when these three features begin to intertwine and interact. It thrives in environments where universities have adopted models of strategic planning that are informed, strangely enough, by the same traditional Western ways of understanding that many in university life have come to see, through various forms of postmodernist critique and comparative studies, as deeply problematic. Beginning with Plato and Aristotle, Western thought came to be largely structured by the idea that things of this world are only real insofar as they correspond with, or are deduced from, abstract and eternal principles that exist outside of the world. We see this orientation in most contemporary strategic plans, with their establishment of first principles of "mission, vision, and values," followed by deduction and "alignment" of lower principles with the higher. The problematic nature of this epistemology becomes clear once we find that within this frame there is little patience for what some feminists and some champions of democracy call "reflexivity," the capacity of "lower" practices to trigger refinement of "higher" principles. As a consequence, there is blindness to the emergent design that is integral to genuine inquiry, the capacity to revise in process rather than having everything unfold on schedule from a preset plan. Correspondence epistemologies also effectively prohibit the discovery of something new, which is often taken to be the essential point of distinction between education and training. The tendency is rather for the strategic plan and its accompanying assessment program to push relentlessly downward through the curriculum and, via objectives, goals, measures, rubrics and data, into the syllabus, bringing closure, standardization, and almost inevitably the pedagogy famously identified by Paulo Freire as "the banking model."³

René Descartes, usually understood to be the founder of modern philosophy, took the correspondence paradigm one step further. He doubted everything of "body"—such as unwritten understandings, history, local wisdom—until he could clear the slate and get to a "clear and distinct idea." This allowed him to sever any vital connection with the world, thereafter relating to it on the terms of abstraction only, leaving out everything not comprehended by the abstract construction, and accepting no new input from fresh experience. The way of being that issued from this orientation—commonly known as Cartesianism—effectively relegates all perceptions other than those of the abstract ideas to the category of "something else," something irrelevant and/or annoying.

Contemporary managers reflect Cartesianism and the mind-body dichotomy, as they are increasingly able to insulate themselves from the ambiguities and challenges of the classroom—and thereby also from teaching as an art, through the granting of administrative status and/or "released time" for managerial duties. Annoyance with the unavoidable complexities of genuine teaching and learning is expressed as insistence that educational relationships submit to the scientific paradigm, with increasingly aggressive response to any who would question or depart from this submission. Meanwhile, the ways in which this insistence distorts, constrains, and even violates our embodied relationships with students, are not noticed. This is especially true in the humanities, where friendliness and helpfulness in relation to difficult course material can never be a substitute for educational encounter. It is truly stunning that, after a century of severe self-criticism and deconstruction of traditional and modern Western culture, we do not recognize this Cartesian process at work in our universities as the same colonization that was exported all over the globe with devastating consequences, and is now applied to our own best practices and cultural dignity. Perhaps managerial colonization of our universities today should be seen as some kind of perverse penance.

Managerialism signals the next stage in the modern process of the rationalization of everything. It is problematic because, while rationalization brings many good things (airplanes, surgeries, efficiencies, and so on), it also entails mechanization and alienation, the "iron cage" of which Max Weber spoke. The problem with managerialism, and with modernity generally, is that humans are easily seduced by the benefits of mechanization, but do not thrive within the closed systems that are inherent to it. We wind up with what Martin Luther King, Jr. referred to as "guided missiles but misguided men [sic]."[4] Humans need openness, possibility, adventure, all of which are closed down by mechanism.

In order for humans to thrive, we need direct participation in the kind of energy that leads some religionists to speak of us as created "in God's image," as creators or co-creators, beings capable of the creativity and innovation that makes Western liberal education so attractive, for example, in China and India. In Hannah Arendt's more Greek and secular terms, we only become fully human within "the paradoxical plurality of unique beings," and an environment that is friendly to "action," as revelation of our uniqueness as a "who" rather than a "what."[5] When this basic human capacity is choked off by mechanism, no matter how wonderful the benefits that might otherwise accrue, humans whither and suffer what T. S. Eliot spoke of as death "not with a bang but with a whimper,"[6] the death of gradual and often pleasant diminution, or "sleep of empire."

Maybe this humanistic language is too exotic for our time. I can make the same point by reference to an excellent book on the history of American public education and strategic planning. Jal Mehta, in his *The Allure of Order,* argues that the failure of American public education arises from the mistaken application of scientific management and the techniques of industry in the attempt to achieve order and control through rationalizing education. This attempt inevitably fails because education is fundamentally relational, a matter of who we are, not as mechanism but, again, as human beings. What is needed, according to Mehta, is a more professional structure where "the emphasis is less on control and regulation than on creating structures in which talented, frontline practitioners can learn from one another and develop and spread new ideas."[7] The limits of strategic planning, as distinct from the wishful thinking it fuels, are all the more dramatic — and ironic — when we consider the remarkable lack of evidence as to its efficacy, as Edward Miech and others have pointed out.[8]

Really, we are talking about two very different paradigms, two different understandings of articulation, embodiment, and their relation — and maybe even the breakdown of the Cartesian worldview as a new one is beginning to emerge. In one paradigm/worldview, articulation is the prior activity, as it has been in much of the history of Western culture. And because it sees embodiment as only a matter of application, articulation tends to be static, a settled doctrine that then initiates the deductive process of implementation. It has the advantage of simplicity. The other vision is more circular and more relational, welcoming ongoing refinement of both articulation and embodiment, and inclining less toward hierarchy and more toward democratic community. The first favors control, stability, and moves toward training, the second toward discovery, reflexivity, and continuous growth in the cultivation of higher order human capacities.[9] The first is closed, the second is open. Education in our time has become a focal point for conflict between these two paradigms, a conflict that will likely have profound consequences for the future.

The fundamental distinction between control/order and production, on the one hand, and practical wisdom or judgment (Greek *phronesis*, practical wisdom; Indian *upaya*, skillful means; Chinese *wu wei*, action of non-action) on the other, brings us to the question as to what we can do to moderate overemphasis on the former and support the latter in our time of constriction and fear. Those of us who are committed to the transformative power of education as necessary to a free society must remain open to the vitality that flows from continuous efforts to articulate and embody our ineffable ideal of the educated person. We need to remember that an ideal can never be reduced to a doctrine; it is an entity about which there is more than one right answer, where each answer is approximate and contingent on the circumstances from which it arises. In fact, this, in itself, can be seen as a definition of the education, maturity, and worldview we seek: the liberal education of coming to the developed ability to be at home in the dialogical life (or "the examined life," per 38a of Socrates' *Apology*) wherein one becomes capable of engaging with both other and self in relation to entities such as "quality," "education," and "democracy," and enjoying the benefits that flow from the pluralistic environment. We need to teach our students and administrators — and each other, again and again — how to live and move and thrive within the complexity and dynamism that are actual to our situation, honoring the sense in which education is a lifelong function of not only accomplishment but also hygiene.

It helps in this honoring to know that we are not alone, that there are others out there who are advocating and embodying an alternative to managerialism that is consistent with the second paradigm or worldview. Here the work of the Association for Contemplative Mind in Higher Education, the YESplus Program, and the conference on "Uncovering the Heart of Higher Education," noted in the previous chapter, are especially helpful.

Staying in touch with those others who share the alternative paradigm — and who realize that the choice before us today is ultimately at this level — can help us maintain awareness of 1) the fine and utterly crucial line between strategic planning/assessment as the wedge through which managerialism enters and colonizes, and 2) the opportunity for democratic leadership and process. This awareness can help us remain open to the possibility that strategic planning and assessment are not necessarily tied to hierarchy and number, an essential possibility since there is no way we can or should seek exemption from the requirements of accountability and continuous improvement. Faculty protests involving cynical withdrawal only cede power to the managers, confirming them in their disdain for faculty and validating their wish to replace professors with service providers (whether in the form of prepackaged, machine-delivered lectures or contingent faculty).

We must, then, do what we have done in previous eras of challenge, and that is to step up and meet a new constraint with the persuasiveness of our ideal, communicating with the public through results that do not always comport with the sometimes crude assessment instruments imposed upon us. We must remain faithful to our students and the dignity of practices we know to be conducive to their well-being and best development, turning strategic planning/assessment constraints into ways we can refine and expand our work, and thereby provide "data" more rich than had been hoped for. Along with our students, we need to continue moving, even against strong headwinds, toward more complete embodiment of our ambitious ideal of the educated citizen. This is our best hope for the modern experiment with democracy and the cultivation of the more developed form of adulthood our era so urgently requires. For the change we seek needs to come not from the top down, but from the bottom up, through the integrity of our encounter with each student. Sticking with this vocation, of course, requires keeping the faith that there may be more power generated by the educational encounter than we are presently able to perceive.

ENDNOTES

1   Originally published in *Liberal Education* 100.3 (Summer 2014).

2   Stephen Toulmin, *Cosmopolis: The Hidden Agenda of Modernity* (Chicago: University of Chicago Press, 1990).

3   Paulo Freire, *The Pedagogy of the Oppressed* (New York: Continuum, 1998).

4   Martin Luther King, Jr., *Where Do We Go From Here: Chaos or Community?* (Boston: Beacon Press, 1968), 172.

5   Hannah Arendt, *The Human Condition* (Chicago: University of Chicago Press, 1958), 176, 179.

6   T. S. Eliot, Choruses from 'The Rock' in *The Complete Poems and Plays: 1909-1950* (New York: Harcourt, Brace and Co., 1952), 96.

7   Jal Mehta, *The Allure of Order: High Hopes, Dashed Expectations, and the Troubled Quest to Remake American Schooling* (New York: Oxford University Press, 2013), 270.

8   Edward Miech, "The Rise and Fall of Strategic Planning and Strategic Planning in Education," *Harvard Educational Review* 65.3 (1995): 504.

9   Martha Nussbaum, *Not for Profit: Why Democracy Needs the Humanities* (Princeton: Princeton University Press, 2010).

3

REDISCOVERING LIBERAL EDUCATION IN CHINA

An Essay on the Benefits of Dialogue and Inquiry[1]

I'M THINKING OF THAT MOMENT WHEN ALL IS ALIGNED just right and your boat glides along in perfection, when wind and wave and set of sail come into harmonious relation, as though another quality is entering in and takes over. I have experienced something like this in education, and it is to me one of the most beautiful events that can occur on this planet: the actual event of education, liberal education as one of the world's great transformative practices. It is quite distinct from training, informing, schooling, equipping, and all the other things that approximate and are thereby mistaken for liberal education.

I have spoken of this moment in terms of a synergy between substance and process elements, between material taught and student initiative through which that material is taken in, integrated with previous learnings, and put to some good use. It is when the substance of education—the stuff of it, the knowledge, ideas, and texts—comes into proper alignment with the process or method and relationality of it—the activities of inquiry, reading, and writing—that the desired experience is most likely to occur.

This articulation has functioned for me as a working understanding in the practice of teaching,[2] and also as a diagnostic screen on which to account for challenges and failures of education. For example, when we look at our era, we see that substance was *given* in the past in the form of the canon, and that in our post-traditional era the substance aspect is either absent or confused. The old canon has been deconstructed, relativized, and augmented to the point where — apart from a canon of famous counter-canon critiques, explicitly conservative islands of tradition, and idiosyncratic reconstructions — agreements about the substance side of education are virtually non-existent.

This accounts, at least in part, for the fact that most articulations of education in America today are set way on the process side, as the development of capacities or virtues. So education is understood as a developmental process that generates specifically human capacities that do not ordinarily arise except through the cultivation of what used to be called a "second nature." Chief and most general among these is "critical thinking," with "civic virtue" following closely.[3] These indicate the ability to not only understand an argument, but to evaluate it against other actual or potential arguments, thereby identifying their relative strengths and weaknesses, and then moving beyond understanding and evaluation to formulation of recommendations as to the best course of action in the matter at hand. It is through guided exercise of these higher order mental capacities[4] — understanding, evaluating, and recommending — in the protected and enriched environment of the classroom, that we develop the ability to live them in the broader worlds of personal, professional, and civic life.

However, articulation of the process approach proves to be easier than the actual doing of it. Too often, and with too little acknowledgment in the American discussion about higher education today, the process orientation, while seeking to support developmental movement, can slip off into an unintended enabling of that which its champions otherwise find noxious. Too often students learn a superficial rhetoric and behavior of the virtues approach—with discussion-oriented classes, valuing of individual experience, collaborative projects, and papers (not exams)—and trick both themselves and their teachers into thinking something deeper is going on. What we have in reality, however, is the further entitling of already over-entitled consumers who thereby become more deeply entrenched in their isolated and anointed individualism.[5] Entitlement and isolation are accompanied by the assumption that we all have an opinion and that ours is as good as any other. This leads to the instability of hypercritical and cynical attitudes toward commitments, principles, and any kind of authority,[6] which, strangely, can flip over into naïve accommodation to learning the procedures and techniques of whatever organizations are perceived to offer opportunity.[7] Perhaps at a deeper level the process orientation gone astray becomes a curriculum of nihilism, teaching that life in the world is about nothing more than power and the arts of calculated advantage, manipulation, and unbridled competition—accompanied by a superficial and purely instrumental friendliness.

Experience of this vexing package of contemporary student attitudes will be familiar to anyone who spends time in classrooms, as distinct from the think tanks and faculty seminars where most of the virtue-oriented programs are generated. The experience of contemporary students drives back to Socrates' most paradoxical proclamation: that one thing he really knows—apart from "knowing nothing"—is that knowledge is always better than opinion, even correct opinion, because knowledge is "tied down," grounded in substance, and hence not susceptible to being blown around on the sea of opinions, preferences, and false notions, washing up on the beaches of lands very far from those of truth and wisdom.[8] How is virtue, as opposed to mere empowerment, possible in an environment where everything slides around? Where can we find anything like reliable substance, some *grounding* for education in the world of today?

GOING TO CHINA PERPLEXED

Awash in these perplexities, an invitation arrived to consult on the development of general education in China. This, on the face of it, seemed improbable: an invitation from Shanghai Jiao Tong University (SJTU, or Jiao Da) in Shanghai, an excellent and very influential university, but one focused strongly on science and technology, and a *Chinese* university at that—where the Ministry of Education in Beijing prescribes as general education a series of courses centered on Party doctrine.

What they wanted by way of consultation with me was precisely "critical thinking" and the contemporary process-oriented cultivation of virtues, as distinct from the content-defined type of education. Like other Chinese universities, SJTU reflects a generalized awareness that China cannot succeed in the new millennium by continuing to do what it did in the Deng Xiaoping era of imitation and replication within a "socialist market economy"; that the "China model" must include innovation, invention, and generation of "the next thing." It must include something like liberal education.[9] In initial phases of the relationship with SJTU colleagues via email and Skype, we agreed that the best general education program would be centered on "cultivation of the developed capacities for critical thinking, creative problem-solving, and responsible innovation."

I was happy to accept the invitation, having previously experienced the creativity of dialogue with China, and was committed to a future in which we could be partners and friends rather than adversaries.[10]

Before going, I had my doubts. I wondered how, in practical terms, it could be possible to actually reform existing Chinese general education. Break the big Party-generated lecture courses down into smaller groups where a process-oriented, liberal education pedagogy of "active learning" could be introduced? This would be problematic, since doctrine is, after all, doctrine. The other approach would be to add courses. In our correspondence, they proposed the following list of courses as possible additions to the Jiao Da General Education curriculum: "Introduction of Logic: Training of Thinking and Reasoning," "Introduction of Epistemology and Science Philosophy: Traditional Analysis of Knowledge, Pragmatic and Marxist," "Introduction of Comparative Philosophy: A Comparative Research of Ethics Between Western and China," and "Introduction of Comparative Political Economy: Neo-Liberalist and Marxist." This identification was mysterious to me at first. How did these topics address the perceived need?—or what did they reveal about it? Looking again, I saw how strongly the comparative dimension is present in this list, and took this as possible openness to dialogue as that form in which comparison moves beyond static debate to dynamic and fruitful relationship.[11]

Then I went. Being there, I was immersed in the genial flow of meetings and meals that are the media of consultation in Shanghai, where stops for decision tend to be either quite formal or extremely subtle from an American perspective. It occurred to me early on how completely opposite our situations really are. They are so substance-oriented, and we are so process-oriented in this era. But then I had a thought: are we so invested on the process side in the U.S. that we fail to notice the emergence of an inadvertent post-traditional kind of substance defined by the conjunction of technological capacity, organizational procedure, market analysis, and individual preference? Could these values be seen as the peculiar catholicity of our time—at least in the West—possibly as inherent to the modern value-set as it appears and progressively overshadows any human culture? Our substance is, in many ways, process itself,[12] and one that is unexamined and confused.

China, in a way, is more "traditional"[13] in that Chinese colleagues live in an environment of massive substance that is given by the Party and is not negotiable. Like "traditional education"[14] in the West, Chinese colleagues live with the constraints of an established canon, as well as the ever-present possibility of its enforcement in the face of actual or potential rebellion. The concern with these constraints is understandable, despite widespread acknowledgment in the university that the constraints of the Party are probably necessary to maintain order, along with a sense that the Chinese Communist Party (CCP) is becoming more liberal from within. This vague sense of legitimacy, in combination with a new Chinese confidence associated with both revival of traditional Chinese culture and contemporary market success, function to provide a sort of enclosure within the Chinese university—an enclave of confidence and optimism to which I do not have access. I cannot say exactly what is going on in this enclosure, any more than any Westerner can account for the vitality of China, apart from that mentioned above. China is an incubator of great energy. There is *power* in the Chinese university,[15] a cultural and personal quality quite distinct from the threat of physical pain associated with mere force. But it is an indeterminate potentiality, energy that could be released and made concrete in a number of quite different directions. Anxiety of the Party and the world—and the Chinese people—about the future of China seems well-founded. And yet at the same time Chinese interest in not only reformed general education but in liberal education as well is genuine, even among those who are party officials within the university—strange and confusing as this may seem to Americans. Even more significant, I think, is the Chinese willingness toward comparative and even dialogical engagement.

Awareness of the mysterious vitality in Chinese universities led me to wonder: is there a hidden vitality to Western liberal education as well? It occurred to me that there is. Beyond cynicism and nihilism, the corporatization of higher education, devaluing of the humanities in favor of STEM (science, technology, engineering, math) disciplines, and the domination of market economy in American universities, there is at the same time a renewed and perhaps more mature appreciation of the greatness of the Western tradition of liberal education.[16] Beyond the inadvertent and problematic substance I mentioned before, there is a step toward more full embodiment of the liberal ideal in America. This is exemplified by the very critical thinking movement I have been discussing, and by the great influence of the Association of American Colleges and Universities in American higher education at this point historically, assuming what used to be the position of Harvard and the University of Chicago as setters and adjusters of the canon. Here, it seems to me, we have something very basic to our era. At the same time the post-traditional catholicity just described can be so problematic, we also see sources of strength and revival. This recalls an especially clear statement about the nature of our era from the great sociologist Robert N. Bellah: "the very situation that has been characterized as one of the collapse of meaning and the failure of moral standards can also, and I would argue more fruitfully, be viewed as one offering unprecedented opportunities, for creative innovation in every sphere of human action."[17]

To affirm the process side of education as the primary source of its vitality is not to ignore what Socrates said about the need for things to be "tied down" in knowledge, rather than wagging in mere opinion. Rather, my point is that, at bottom, liberal education, though it certainly needs the substance aspect, is really more like a transformative practice than it is correctness of thought, more praxeology than doctrine.[18] The root of this fine distinction — especially fine since in liberal education the medium of practice is thought, and hence most easily confused with the mere exchange of theories, as the martial arts in China are most easily confused with mere fighting — can be seen in *Phaedo* 114d, where Socrates, after experimenting with several formulations in thought about the necessity of affirming the immortality (or existence!) of the soul, finally pulls back and says:

> No sensible man [*sic*] would insist that these things are as I have described them, but I think it is fitting for a man to risk the belief — for the risk is a noble one — that this, or something like this, is true about our souls and their dwelling places, since the soul is evidently immortal, and a man should

repeat this to himself as if it were an incantation, which is why I have prolonged my tale.[19]

His orientation to what we believe is modest and functional.

In this understanding of education, the work of the intellect is not to capture, contain, and transmit absolute truth, but to remind us again and again of the nobility of risking belief—or we might say conscious affirmation—and to provide a safe and resource-rich environment in which to examine, test, and exercise those beliefs, values, and commitments that constitute our affirmation. Here we find an orientation to thought very different from that of the doctrine prevalent in the traditional West after the canonization of Plato and Aristotle, and one that is quite friendly to process values and transformation. It perhaps requires more from us than was required by the old canon orientation. It perhaps requires us to become pragmatists and acknowledge that appropriate knowledge/substance can vary according to the problem or question under inquiry. And insofar as becoming pragmatists entails an honoring of the concrete particularities of living a contingent life, it also requires revival of the old Greek notion of *phronesis*, practical judgment, judgment in the particulars of life in support of ongoing transformative process.

But let us take note of the fact that these reflections do not really, or at least directly, address the question about the substance side of education. Also, pursuit of them could lead us away from the conversation in Shanghai. So I want to return to the adventure at SJTU, noting at this point that the vitality of relationship with China is that, as much as it is helpful in terms of understanding the other, it pushes us to fresh awareness of what is great in our own tradition as well.

DIALOGUE AND DISCOVERY

At a certain point the conversation in Shanghai about what would constitute an adequate general education began to congeal around an understanding about the problematic nature of the society for which we are preparing our students. We began to focus on modernity, and the understanding that the modern values to which both of our societies are attuned are not sustainable. They are, in fact, not even all that desirable once they are brought out of the fog of addictive attachment and into the light of critical awareness. More specifically, we together saw the stark contrast between modern friendliness toward machines and its almost complete disregard for the human dimension, except insofar as it can be bent toward machine function. Perhaps this disregard of the human occurred while people were under the illusion of Western individualism, which assumes that the human dimension is a purely private matter. And perhaps adoption of Western individualism occurs as a kind of oversight when people are so enthusiastic about other, more positive values of modernity: not only higher levels of material well-being, but also democracy/pluralism, the integrity of individual experience, and the possibility of liberation and growth. No matter how it happened, though, the degraded view of the human as the isolated individual defined by nothing more than rights to privacy and material possession came to be interwoven into the global meaning of modernization (and its near identity with Americanization).[20] Hence, critical awareness of modernity becomes awareness of having been held captive to those values that followed from that individualism as it played out in modern history: competition, commodification, homogenization, and reduction—and a systematic overlooking of any need to cultivate the person as a human being.[21]

This coming to awareness of a commonly shared problem was all the more vivid for our now being able to view it together from two sides of the same planet.[22] This existential awareness, beyond merely intellectual claims about modernity's limitations—which is nothing new on either side—began to open up an atmosphere of educational possibility, including a sense that liberation from our shared condition of oppression might actually occur. In fact, it seemed to be occurring just then, in our meeting on the eleventh floor of the Humanities Building at Jiao Tong.

Two other insights followed. First, it was pointed out that awakening to the insufficiencies of the modern, to its unsustainable and undesirable qualities, often happens when people are morally and spiritually exhausted, and hence susceptible to desperate measures, like those associated with fundamentalism, reactionary movements, or even terrorist lashing out. Second, it was observed that our act of discovering the insufficiency of the modern together seemed to open up accessibility to the wisdom of the very traditions—in this instance, Chinese and Western—that modernity had dismissed and despised. It was as though the pavement had cracked and something that had been covered over by modern values was now coming up from the ground. Could the humanly shared problem of modernity's limitations, and the availability of resources with which to address them in the depths of the world's great civilizations, provide the substance we so badly need in order to stabilize and "tie down" education?

Maybe this is too dramatic. The point, though, is availability: that resources from the great traditions of the Axial Period[23] begin to be available in fresh ways after we together come to acknowledge the limits of modernity. More specifically, tradition begins to be available as repository of wisdom on the most urgent matter at hand; that is, the cultivation of the mature or fully formed human being.[24] Here we also have protection against fundamentalism and rigid traditionalisms, since cultivation—especially insofar as it occurs in the presence of others who are paradoxically different in the traditions they search and yet the same in the agenda of searching—provides a principle by which to identify and select from that which is great in our traditions, while leaving behind those completely unacceptable values by which they were carried through history in the Post-Axial Period, namely, their racism, classism, sexism, etc.

With these insights, Western people like myself have a new lens to look through, as well as a new reason to see what is worth saving in the West. In an unstable atmosphere of Western flipping back and forth between arrogant assertion and self-deprecating critique, this is an urgent matter. The encounter with friends from China helps us see that the Western inheritance need not be only the imposition of the intellectual systems that so enchanted our ancestors. Rather, we can see Socrates in the *Apology,* astonished that people cared so little for the state of their souls and insisting that excellence through living the "examined life" is the only reliable source of a healthy life, not fame and fortune.[25] We come to a fresh appreciation of Aristotle, not in his establishment of deductive certainty and the closed intellectual system in the *Metaphysics,* but through his more concrete efforts in the *Ethics* to guide us to virtue, not by constructing theories of the good, but by helping us to *become* good. We do this by pursuing goodness as a practical mean between excess and defect, through habituating actions that are conscious, undertaken for their own sake rather than for some instrumental good they might secure, and persistent.[26]

I see Chinese colleagues doing something similar. In recent years, to cite a dramatic example, Peimin Ni has suggested that the reason traditional Chinese philosophy has been dismissed in the West (and the East as well in the century since China internalized Western values) as vague, fluid, and/or impossibly poetic is that it is written from a perspective quite different from that of Western philosophy. Most philosophy in the West is written from the perspective of theory construction, as a linear progression of propositional truth and logical argument, culminating in irresistible conclusions. In the East, according to Ni, philosophy is written from the perspective of supporting human development, from the perspective of *gongfu*[27] or cultivation. Hence it appears strange through the Western lens. The following statement from Confucius in the *Analects,* for example, and as cited by Ni, reveals very clearly the Confucian developmental vision of movement toward becoming a fully mature human being:

> From fifteen, my heart-and-mind was set upon learning; from thirty I took my stance; from forty I was no longer

doubtful; from fifty I realized the propensities of *tian (tianming)* [heaven; mandate of heaven]; from sixty my ear was attuned; from seventy I could give my heart-and-mind free reign without overstepping the boundaries.[28]

Is this not a very helpful illumination of the developmental path through which human beings come to that state of "free reign without overstepping" that we acknowledge as maturity? Is this not that capacity we admire in Chinese culture as *wu wei* (action of non-action)? Let us transliterate a bit: becoming set in a certain seriousness or engagement in life, taking a "stance" as a healthy position or commitment, coming to a centered sort of confidence and liberation from distracting self-consciousness, experience of being aligned in one's presence with a higher order of reality, being able to sustain this alignment, and finally being able to live and act without distraction.

But it is essential to emphasize that this kind of reappropriation, either of the riches of the other's tradition or one's own, does not occur through a static comparative approach, but only through the relational dynamism and more complex process we know as dialogue.[29] This is to say that access to the developmental riches of my own tradition and actualization of those riches occurs most effectively in the presence of those from other traditions who are doing something similar. Here is a point that is utterly basic to the positive potential of our era: dialogue is experienced as solution to the root challenge or riddle of our suddenly global situation, that of unity and diversity. In dialogue, both are affirmed simultaneously, no longer one at the expense of the other, no longer the either/or of unity, which is hegemonic and/or homogenizes and annihilates diversity, versus diversity, which opens onto chaos. Through the paradox of actual dialogical relationship, a new experience of universality occurs. It is not the old Western universality of achieving the superior position above and beyond the conflict of opposed particularity, but rather an experience of profound commonality that opens up in the depth of particularity. It occurs when we listen to and question the Other in the depth of their own particularity, at the same time they do the same for us, in pursuit of solution to commonly shared problems and issues of life on a very finite planet. The paradox of dialogue shows the way beyond the otherwise impossible contradictions and irreconcilable oppositions of the present.[30]

BACK TO JIAO TONG, THEN HOME

I hope all this wondering about renewed vitality, and the reappropriation of my own tradition that it has entailed, as well as admiration of my colleagues' reappropriation, has not caused me to stray too far away from those hot September days at Jiao Tong. Something remarkable happened there. As the conversation about general education went on, past the point about modernity as a commonly shared problem, and then awareness that the great traditions of the Axial Age contain as their deepest riches wisdom to address the problem, it became a splendid and highly educative exercise in dialogue itself.

Reappropriation of my own tradition as a resource for human development occurred. In the presence of Chinese colleagues I found myself able to speak with surprising clarity about Socrates. This includes some of the things I have already reported about liberal education as practice rather than doctrine, and "belief" as conscious affirmation rather than either demonstrable logical proposition or complete surrender to authority. At another point the meaning of *Apology* 38a came into greater focus than ever before:

> I tell you that to let no day pass without discussing goodness and all the other subjects about which you hear me talking and examining both myself and others is really the very best thing a man [*sic*] can do, and that a life without this sort of examination is not worth living.[31]

Philosophy is a daily hygiene of coming to "know nothing," letting go of false or merely egotistical knowings, which, at the same time, opens us up to our "divine sign" or "inner voice."[32]

And on the Chinese side as well: the colleague who cited the Confucius passage about "following my heart's desire" later cited the six classical arts of Chinese culture—rituals, music, archery, charioteering, calligraphy, and mathematics—as fundamentally oriented to cultivation of the person rather than as mere technical skills on the one hand, or entertainments on the other. Another reappropriation occurred by way of a fresh and distinctly Chinese reading of Marx.[33]

When I reflected later on this dialogical event, I was struck by how different many Chinese colleagues and contexts are now from what they had been when my own back-and-forth with China began nearly two decades ago, spurred on by the need to "internationalize" American higher education. In the early nineties, most Chinese philosophy and humanities departments were scrambling to keep up with the latest Western trend, especially in analytical philosophy and Jacques Derrida's deconstruction. But then, apparently in some part due to the impact of the intercultural dialogue movement[34] and renewed interest of people from outside of China in the riches of Chinese tradition, things began to change. Chinese colleagues began to be less willing to merely accept the latest Western thing and more interested in real engagement and articulation of their own integrity. Leaders like Tu Weiming emerged with articulation of the deep dignity of the Chinese tradition in eloquent English, and in vivid comparison with the world's leading cultural and philosophical influences. A whole movement arose to present the efficacy of Confucianism in relation to crises that are global in nature.[35]

Likewise, Western engagement in the past two decades has moved from tendencies toward romanticizing ancient China and criticizing everything Western as hegemonic, based on false and chauvinistic universalizing, essentializing, etc. These proclivities have given way in recent years to much greater capacity for realistic assessment of China, as well as some greater ability to speak about what is great in the West, often in terms of Socrates, pragmatism, process philosophy, feminism, and the Frankfort School.

I returned to the U.S., then, with real learning in terms of refinement of American higher education, specifically in terms of how to facilitate cultivation of virtues without such a high risk of having the effort fall into the nihilistic degradation that describes so much of the broader cultural environment in which we teach. I had rediscovered the value of the problem/issue/question/task approach associated with progressive education, now in relation to three tasks that can be seen as most general to our global present: 1) to understand the senses in which modernity is corrosive to our humanity and a problem that is commonly shared by all modernized societies;[36] 2) to discover resources within one or more of the world's great traditions that address the cultivation of the human being in ways that are, paradoxically, both the same as and different from other ways across the planet; and 3) to "reappropriate" those resources through dialogue with persons from other traditions who are (again, paradoxically) doing the same.[37] These tasks, again as the most basic challenge for education and culture today, provide an outline for general education. Further elaboration of this interdisciplinary (or post-disciplinary) vision of general education can be seen in relation to the overwhelming issues we need developed human beings to address, issues like sustainability, human and environmental rights, and the deployment of technological resources. The possibility I am recommending is that through the dialogue between and among traditions in/as the full plurality of the multicultural life we share, it will be possible to engage that particular tradition of cultivation that we know ambiguously on a worldwide basis as "education" or "higher education."[38]

Insofar as the problem-centered approach is engaged in the mode of dialogue—as it was at Jiao Da, and as it sometimes is not, for example, in some business, industrial, military, and educational settings[39]—it can be seen as involving a revival of liberal education as well. Begin with a commonly shared task, or question, or problem (the "other subjects" in Socrates' statement; i.e., not just a problem of consumer preference, etc., but a *real* problem) that serves to initiate inquiry. Examine "both myself and others" as to the best path to solution. Introduce sources from outside of the immediate working group that can inform and support the inquiry, then move to solutions—hoping, but not insisting, that some consensus or mutual discovery will emerge. Does this not include both process and substance aspects, now held together and apart by the dynamic interplay of inquiry?

Dialogue between our partners in inquiry, and the sources we have selected as significant to the problem at hand, constitute the learning environment within which the desired qualities of critical thinking and civic virtue can be generated, those qualities that could never be taught in abstraction from inquiry as free floating techniques or "skills."[40] If inquiry or practice of "the examined life" goes well, opinion and simple individual preference are transformed into something more like the "knowledge" Socrates was talking about, as they are refined in dialogue with the otherness of partners in inquiry. In this way both substance and process aspects of education find discipline and direction through our mutual commitment to addressing the problem—again, the problem as an embodiment of the life we share.

It is essential to this learning that it comes not only through our own primary engagement with tasks or problems/issues/questions, but also that it occurs with others who are likewise engaged. It should not be through application of pre-determined theories, dogmas, or procedures, as in pre-formulated textbooks and syllabi. Inquiry and emergent design become necessary to the integrity of liberal education in the global age.[41] They also point toward a way in which the university could become "universal"—not in the sense of embracing all subject matter, but in becoming a model for society and the problem-solving capacity it so urgently needs. The university in this sense could even provide the worldwide ground (and a method and some resources) upon which real actors and stakeholders might convene to address those most urgent issues upon which the future depends. This understanding could even give rise to a global consortium of universities and an expanded appreciation of what the university can and should be.

My own laboratory experience of this kind of learning with Chinese colleagues demonstrates, above all, that there is no need for opposition between the process and substance aspects of learning, or between practice and theory, or the experiential and ideational dimensions, as in so much of Western history, including the history of education. It is not necessary to resolve the tensions by insisting on the priority of theory and absolutized conceptual order as a prerequisite for getting started—or, as Western history occasionally presents as the nihilistic alternative, the reduction of all to either technique or emotion. We Westerners especially need to recognize and affirm quality in the process and experiential dimension—those events, activities, and relationships in which goodness, thriving, and valuable deliberation occur.[42] And we need to support them in forms of interpretation and identification of best practices, so as to maximize the possibility of their occurring again, hopefully ever more broadly and deeply. We need to get past the intellectualism that dominated the West in the historic period, alternating sometimes with its opposite, as expressed in sensationalist, romantic, or shallow, uncritically empiricist movements, causing Western ancestors to be at a loss when it comes to effective affirmation of life in the experiential/developmental dimension. This has made it very difficult to support what we otherwise announce as our most cherished ideals, including democracy, community, healthy interpersonal relationship, liberal education, and other relational arts.

Encounter with the Other, which many of the great cultural and philosophical thinkers of our era identify as the locus of vitality and direction, is key. For here we have the opportunity to grow beyond our historic deficit. Chinese others, for example—and *by example*—can help us find some greater measure of comfort and at-homeness in the immediacy of lived-life, and confidence that some greater trusting of the gift quality of life need not cause us to drift off into incoherence, thereby provoking defensive retreat into ever more rigid abstraction. They can introduce us to some historic figures from the Chinese tradition who model healthy ways of balancing the experiential and the ideational, and letting the ideational serve the experiential rather than dominating, distorting, and obscuring the wisdom and energy that are present there. They can help us to identify and value resources in our own tradition through which we can grow in the direction of living that healthy balance, and even, on occasion, sailing into that mysterious quality that allows us to give the "heart-mind free reign."

We, in turn, might help them too, and there are signs that this may be occurring. But this would be impossible for me to say, beyond a generalized trust in our relationship. I await our next meeting with anticipation and hope.

ENDNOTES

1   Originally published in *Soundings: An Interdisciplinary Journal* (Spring 2013).

2   See my "Access to a Vision: Unlocking the Paradox of Liberal Education," in Stephen Rowe, ed. *Claiming a Liberal Education: Resources for Realizing the College Experience* (Needham Heights, MA: Ginn Press, 1992) and *Overcoming America/America Overcoming: Can We Survive Modernity?* (Lanham, MD: Lexington Books, 2012).

3   On the prominence of these process values, see the very influential Association of American Colleges and Universities (AAC&U), especially its Liberal Education and America's Promise (LEAP) program.

4   For early articulation of this development, see Benjamin Bloom, *Taxonomy of Educational Objectives: The Classification of Educational Goals* (New York: McKay, 1956). See also William Perry, *Forms of Moral and Intellectual Development in the College Years* (New York: Holt, Rinehart, and Winston, 1968).

5   Here, it seems to me, is the typical liability of the process and virtue oriented-approach to education, which I myself advocate:

the liability of cooptation to problematic forms of Western individualism. Note that John Dewey, America's strongest advocate of progressive education, has been criticized on these terms.

6   In the *Republic,* Socrates speaks of the nearly or imperfectly educated as those who "delight like puppies in pulling about and tearing with words all who come near them." Plato, *Republic,* VII, 539b, in *The Collected Dialogues of Plato,* eds. Edith Hamilton and Huntington Cairns, Bollingen Series, no. 71 (New York: Pantheon Books, 1985), 771.

7   This kind of instability recalls lessons of the French Revolution, as, for example, in Hannah Arendt's telling of them in her *On Revolution* (New York: Viking Press, 1963).

8   Plato, *Meno* 97d-98b, *The Collected Dialogues of Plato,* 381–82.

9   For an insightful report on these trends, see Karen Fischer, "Bucking Cultural Norms, Asia Tried Liberal Arts" in *The Chronicle of Higher Education,* vol. LVIII, no. 23, 10 February 2012, A1, A3–A8.

10 Our department is deeply committed to such a future. We have a summer program in China, and several of our faculty are very active as philosophers in the P.R.C. For my part, two of my books have been translated and published in China, I have attended many conferences there, and have ongoing relationships with several universities and colleagues.

11 On dialogue, see my *Rediscovering the West: An Inquiry into Nothingness and Relatedness* (Albany: SUNY Press, 1994).

12 Pursuing this thought, see Zygmunt Bauman, *Liquid Modernity* (Boston and Cambridge, UK: Polity Press, 2000).

13 It is perhaps a crude distinction, between "modern" and the "traditional" stage that came before, but given the global impact of modern values and modernization, it seems legitimate.

14 In John Dewey's sense of that term in *John Dewey, Experience and Education* (New York: Collier Books, 1963).

15 I speak on the basis of familiarity with not only Jiao Tong, but also East China Normal University, East China University of Science and Technology, Fudan University, and Peking University.

16 For somewhat ironic evidence of renewed appreciation and of how

it arises specifically through the dialogical relationship with Chinese higher education, see Brian P. Coppola and Yong Zhao, "U.S. Education in Chinese Lock Step? Bad Move.," in *The Chronicle of Higher Education,* 10 February 2012, A29–A30.

17 Robert N. Bellah, *Beyond Belief: Essays on Religion in a Post-Traditional World* (New York: Harper & Row, 1970), 44. See also in my *Living Beyond Crisis: Essays on Discovery and being in the World* (New York: Pilgrim Press, 1980), 112.

18 See *Overcoming America / America Overcoming,* 175–77.

19 Plato, *Phaedo* 114d, in *Plato's Phaedo,* ed. G.M.A. Grube (Indianapolis: Hackett, 1977), 64.

20 Now there is strong evidence of awareness of this implicit global meaning, such that choices, alternatives, and "many globalizations" become possible. See Peter L. Berger and Samuel P. Huntington, eds., *Many Globalizations: Cultural Diversity in the Contemporary World* (New York: Oxford University Press, 2002).

21 Of course, critical awareness of modernity in China is different from that of the West, such as my own. It is very important to remember that experience with modernization in China reaches back much further than the recent Deng Xiaoping experiment with "socialist market economy," to the "one hundred years of humiliation," and the career of the May 4 [1919] Movement, culminating in the Cultural Revolution (1966–1976) and establishment of state totalitarianism. My hope is that future meetings with Chinese colleagues can involve more nuanced discussion of differences, including the possibility that I am overly severe in my critique of the Western 17th century natural rights tradition of Hobbes, Locke, and Rousseau as a major source of modernity.

22 I gave a presentation related to this topic on the previous day, and am therefore uncertain as to whether and how deeply this may have influenced the conversation I am reporting on here.

23 Most recently, see Karen Armstrong, *The Great Transformation: The Beginning of Our Religious Traditions* (New York: Alfred A. Knopf, 2006), and Robert N. Bellah, *Religion in Human Evolution: From the Paleolithic to the Axial Age* (Cambridge: Harvard University Press, 2011).

24 On "perennial philosophy" not as a shared metaphysic, but rather as commitment to a method of transformative practice, see, "Dialogue, Development, and Pluralism," Chapter 8 in *Overcoming America /America Overcoming,* 115–26; and Henry Rosemont and Huston Smith, *Is There a Universal Grammar of Religion?* (Chicago: Open Court, 2008).

25 Plato, *Apology* 29d-e, in *The Collected Dialogues of Plato,* 16.

26 Aristotle, *Nicomachean Ethics,* Book II, 4:30, 1105b, in *The Basic Works of Aristotle,* ed. Richard McKeon (New York: Random House, 1941), 956. For others who have come to see Western philosophy from the perspective of development, see Jacob Needleman, *The Heart of Philosophy* (New York: Knopf, 1982) and Pierre Hadot, "Philosophy and Philosophical Discourse," in *What Is Ancient Philosophy?* (Cambridge: Harvard University Press, 2002), 172–233.

27 Peimin Ni, "Kung Fu for Philosophers," in *New York Times,* 8 December 2010, Opinionator.

28 Confucius, *Analects* 2:4, in *The Analects of Confucius,* trans. Roger T. Ames and Henry Rosemont (New York: Ballantine, 1998), 76–77.

29 Note that dialogue indicates both an accomplished developmental stage as well as a practice by which to get there; it both exemplifies and develops higher order mental functions. See Bloom, *Taxonomy of Educational Objectives.*

30 Note the developmental challenge of dialogue for Western people especially, since it requires us to go beyond theory to the ultimacy of a kind of experience which is impossible to articulate without reference to its inherently paradoxical character, a character which has not been well-tolerated by Western philosophy.

31 Plato, *Apology* 38a, in *The Collected Works of Plato,* 23.

32 Ibid., 31d, 40a; 17, 24.

33 For example, Lu Xulong, whose thoughts later came to written articulation in "On the Validity and Invalidity of the Same Evidence Principle: Marxism's Answer to Skeptical Problems and the Gettier Problem,"online: http://ma.sjtu.edu.cn/research/view/148/.

34 See: "Dialogue as Democratic Possibility," Chapter 6 in *Overcoming America /America Overcoming,* 85–101.

35 This movement is known as Third Epoch Confucianism. Representatives who publish in English include Tu Weiming, Henry Rosemont, Peimin Ni, Sor-hoon Tan, Roger Ames, Chenyang Li, David Hall, and Yaming An. For an exemplary work at the foundation of this movement, see Tu Weiming, *Confucian Thought: Selfhood as Creative Transformation* (Albany: SUNY Press, 1985).

36 I don't think this is possible in the mode of simple antimodernism or most of what is called postmodernism in our era. Identifying the positive elements of modernity seems essential, as does keeping in mind the negative elements of tradition. Here I point again to Karen Armstrong's *The Great Transformation* as a model of effective dialogue between traditional and modern vitalities.

37 Upon returning, I read Martha Nussbaum's *Not for Profit: Why Democracy Needs the Humanities* (Princeton: Princeton University Press, 2010), and discovered this work to be a perfect example of comparative general education, of the mutual illumination which can occur when people from different cultures reappropriate the riches of their traditions for human cultivation in dialogue with those from other traditions who are doing the same.

38 Yes, this essay universalizes. But it does so in the distinctly post-traditional way that is discussed above, a way that is pluralistic and even democratic. For a now-classic statement in support of this way of universalizing, see Amartya Sen, "Democracy and Its Global Roots," in *The New Republic*, 6 October 2003, 28–35.

39 In all of these settings, though, there are signs of increased emphasis on less hierarchical management methods which focus on the efficacy of collaboration and teamwork.

40 See, for example, John Henry Newman, *The Idea of a University* (South Bend: University of Notre Dame Press, 1982), on the paradoxical fact that in order for the most desirable qualities to emerge, knowledge must be "its own end," or "an end in itself;" that there is no way of imparting the essential qualities without renouncing the effort to achieve them. This point goes way back to the roots of liberal education in Aristotle's strategy for the cultivation of virtue. Again, see *Nicomachean Ethics*, Book II, 4:30, 1105b.

41 Inquiry-based education requires a structure which, like dialogue, is both open and definite. It needs to be more definite in the beginning

of a course, but more open as inquiry develops; hence, emergent design as an essential quality as well. Note that this kind of education—variously called "progressive," "alternative," "innovative," or even "experimental"—has been very difficult to sustain in the West for the simple reason that alternative structure has been confused with the absence of structure, as the strictly negative understanding of freedom that has so confounded the modern West.

42 A good example of this learning and recognition is presented in Philip Hallie's *Lest Innocent Blood Be Shed: The Story of the Village of Le Chambon and How Goodness Happened There* (New York: Harper Torchbooks, 1979). The earlier work of William James speaks eloquently to the need for a more empirical approach to matters of value, as, for example, in *A Pluralistic Universe:* "Let empiricism once become associated with religion as hitherto, through some strange misunderstanding, it has been associated with irreligion, and I believe that a new era of religion as well as philosophy will be ready to begin." See William James, *Essays in Radical Empiricism and A Pluralistic Universe,* ed. Ralph Barton Perry (New York: Dutton, 1971), 270.

4

THE WORLDVIEW PROBLEM AND DIALOGUE[1]

THERE ARE SO MANY CHALLENGES TO HIGHER EDUCATION in our time that it seems unfair, as though what Fareed Zakaria once described as "America's best industry" has been hobbled. Underneath the well-rehearsed list of challenges associated with demographics, costs, and accountability, it is also important to be aware of the deeper and less discussed challenge of worldview, where "worldview" refers to that largely unconscious, interdependent set of values and paradigmatic experiences in which the whole enterprise is embraced.

The modern American university is rooted in several quite different sources, some of which are associated with the deepest democratic aspirations of the country. But under the stresses of a constricting world in the present, another root source comes to the fore: the Cartesian worldview. Oriented to "value-free" knowledge, competitive individualism, and a world of infinite and essentially inert material resources, this worldview has reached its limit in our time. Collapse of Cartesianism is manifest in two ways. The first is widespread awareness that it is not "sustainable," that continued living in and through this worldview is simply not possible in the global era of limits, interdependence, and equal rights. On top of this awareness a smaller but significant number of people have discovered that the Cartesian lifeway, with its superficial materialism, machine-driven lifestyle, and personal isolation, is not even desirable. The second manifestation of collapse is extreme, nearly fundamentalist, presentation of the basic values of Cartesianism in what I have called "managerialism," indicating a fusion of market rationality, the nihilistic assumption that everything revolves around interest and power, and the modern wish for a clean slate and a new beginning. Through the dominating influence of managerialism, much of the contemporary university is driven by increasingly desperate attempts to address its more immediate challenges through ever more severe application of Cartesian solutions, especially though reduction of all functions to outcomes that can be known through quantitative measure.

But, as I have already indicated, Cartesianism is not the only worldview at work in the American university. Quietly, and from the bottom up rather than the top down, from classrooms and the specifically educational encounters of the university, a relational worldview of the post-Cartesian, global era is rising. This worldview can be characterized briefly as life-affirming, pluralistic, relational, ecologically responsible, and oriented to transformation in the direction of thriving. Because it is pluralistic, it cannot be articulated as a single doctrine or an ideology. And because it is relational, identifying relationship with the other who is and remains different as the locus of thriving, it both requires and generates an order of maturity beyond the either-or world of modernity — either capitalism or communism, individualism or self-sacrifice, etc. Living consciously in the vital dynamic of relationship, the relational worldview is able to appropriate the best features of both traditional culture and modernity, while leaving behind the worst of each, in the ongoing dialogue of what Tu Weiming identifies as a learning culture rather than a teaching culture. As distinct from modernity and its obsession with mechanism, the relational worldview is able to tolerate and even thrive within paradox, a capacity which can be especially threatening to those who are still enveloped in the Cartesian worldview.

Awareness of the co-presence of these very different worldviews, and of higher education as a kind of laboratory—if not a battleground—in the larger society for a momentous historical shift, can help us maintain some perspective on events that can otherwise be sheer frustration. For example, we have great ideas in our midst, like diversity, service, collaboration, inclusion, and civic engagement. But when implementation of these is removed from the hands of committed, front-line professionals in their educational relationships with students, and taken into the Cartesian worldview of managers, they are often coopted to hierarchy, rigid procedures and assessment instruments, and then to the hiring of more managers to do more of the same. The ultimate insult comes when, for example, those who have not taken the manager-designed "inclusion advocacy" training program are assumed by its managerial designers to be racist.

Understanding the "clash of civilizations" (with thanks to Professor Huntington, for his basic and complex observation) that is occurring in our universities can also make it possible for us to focus our efforts, find creative alliances, and locate genuinely "best" practices. It can help us appreciate the possibilities of the co-curricular life of the university—beyond what can appear on some days as a discounting of the classroom and eclipsing it with a second curriculum of endless guest lectures and special events—as a complete and continuous learning environment. It can encourage pedagogical innovation in the movement from subject matter to capacities-based approaches to education, aiming to instill such capacities as Martha Nussbaum's famous three: critical thinking, narrative imagination, and global citizenship. Understanding can open up the implications of recent discoveries in neuroscience and the possibilities of mindfulness and contemplative epistemologies such as are advocated by the Center for Contemplative Mind in Higher Education. It can illuminate the deep significance of the explicitly transformative orientation to education of the whole person, in what Parker Palmer and others have come to call "integrative education." And, finally, awareness of the emerging relational worldview and its radical difference from the Cartesianism enables us to identify and move in the nexus of dynamic overlap between the most vital practices of education in our time. These practices are dialogue and/or comparative education, in which we experience the simultaneous affirmation of two or more parties within the truly democratic encounter; service learning and civic engagement in that mode, where being present for the other can be the most healthy practice for the self; and the state of mindfulness in which we are able to abide in that stillness which is the source of right action.

Keeping in mind the underlying challenge of worldview can also support us in a renewed sense of how we can contribute to the common good. For change at the level of worldview, for better or for worse, is inevitable, and, like the climate change which accompanies it, is already occurring. The fact that education, and liberal education in particular, has historically stressed awareness of worldview as essential to living "the examined life" makes it especially promising in terms of the change we need. For with the emergence of global civilization—through historical consciousness, liberationist movements, and realization of ecological limitations—humans have become alert to culture or worldview like never before, and hence have been pushed across a developmental threshold into a new order of choice and responsibility. So the movement from the Cartesian to the relational worldview depends—as far as we can tell, given our very limited transcendence of history—on conscious recognition of the limited and ultimately lethal qualities of the former, and equally conscious affirmation of the latter, where "conscious" entails the willingness to *live* as though the relational worldview were "true." As we learn through liberal education that neither relativistic individualism nor absolutistic fundamentalism are healthy choices, the relational worldview begins to come into view on the horizon—or sometimes we see it first in the eyes of the other who we really care about. Either way, we finally learn to live to survive modernity to and live in the maturity and vulnerability of beings in whom compassion becomes possible.

Surviving the modern requires a developed awareness of its limiting and ultimately lethal character, an appropriation of sources for the cultivation of human vitality, and activation of these sources through dialogue with those of other traditions who are also addressing the limitations of the modern. This is profoundly different from fundamentalist reaction which asserts "good" tradition against "bad" modernity. It is also quite different from the even more severe lashing out of terrorism. The overcoming I am recommending is a much more nuanced approach that entails conscious affirmation not only of some elements of "tradition," but also of what is valuable in the modern, including the insights of social science.

America is struggling to cross the treacherous ocean over which we find ourselves after humans have been alienated from traditional cultures. Beginning in the late 19th century and intensifying through the 20th, traditions, those age-old containers of human life, have been discovered to be other—amidst wildly mixed feelings of sorrow/loss and critique/anger. Either way, traditional cultures no longer provide a home. We live in the midst of fragments of tradition, as well as desperate attempts to *get back*, to absolutize the order and authority of tradition against the insufficiency of the modern. But fundamentalism never proves to be viable, since it inevitably results in some form of *jihad* against life in the present. However, this does not change the fact that sooner or later the post-traditional, modern confusion does indeed become intolerable. It is the "wasteland" of which T. S. Eliot spoke, a barren ground of unrelenting competition and relativistic indifference to all value except those of number/money, and the consumer preferences of overly entitled but otherwise undistinguished individuals. It is an insult to the human spirit, if not to Dao/Allah/Heaven/God. It is something to be overcome.

In this situation, the deep dilemma of our era becomes one of either absolutism reasserted or relativism unconstrained: either "clash of civilizations," each asserting its own superiority against the modern confusion, or the "end of history" reduction of all to consumerism and the war of all against all. Yet there are also in our midst pockets of beauty and potential, goodness and hope. Some actually do live beyond fanaticism, decadence, and despair; some find a way to cross over to a new ground beyond the limitations of the modern, a way that includes awareness of the largely obscured dignity of America and what is worth saving in the modern Enlightenment project.

Another option becomes available. Most of us have glimpses of it from time to time. There is still something great in America—and in the broader world, something worth standing up for, something beyond just degrees of privilege. The problem is that access to it requires a certain faith and the courage to enter into a developmental process in which vulnerability and openness to growth are necessary. It also requires maintenance of wakefulness in the midst of never-ending modern temptations to narcosis, through lifestyles of multitasking and entertainment, and/or ideologies which insulate against the need to think. Wakefulness, in turn, requires support, confirmation, companionship, nurturance. And it also takes *interpretation*, as the necessary connective tissue between ethereal vision and the embodied presence of ordinary life.

In our time, worldview has become conscious, and hence a matter of choice and responsibility. We experience this, for example, in liberationist movements, environmental awareness, criticisms of capitalist greed and the politics of self-interest, and in calls for inclusion and affirmation of diversity—all of which point to the problematic nature of our inherited worldview and the necessity of change at this level.

But to identify worldview as problem is extremely difficult. In fact, it indicates the sort of difficulty societies of the past did not survive. Worldview is that comprehensive lens through which we apprehend and assign value in all of life, the perspective which informs the way we set priorities, including those having to do with who gives and who receives, how we identify issues and evaluate consequences. For the vast majority of our ancestors, worldview lay beneath conscious awareness, as something given in such a way that it was not seen. The movement beyond the traditional period of human history, as well as movement beyond the crises of our time with which it ends, require that we make conscious that which has been unconscious, choose values that are more life-affirming than those we inherited, *and* act from the perspective of that conscious choice.

Our challenge is nothing less than the reinvention and choosing of the best of *culture itself* under post-traditional circumstances. The imperative is one of growth, and it is inherently religious in nature. It has everything to do with how we orient ourselves in relation to the broadest horizons of meaning and value, and how we are able to transcend ego and draw on energies which lie beyond what we can ordinarily comprehend or control, and yet what we perceive as decisive in our lives. We need religion as William James defined it, as "the belief that there is an unseen order, and that our supreme good lies in harmoniously adjusting ourselves thereto."[1] We need the kind of belief that comes as close as possible to being identical with this "adjusting."

The survival of America — perhaps the world — turns on whether we can become aware of the limitations of the worldview we have inherited, and choose a better one, one more conducive to well-being, more conducive to *life*. America, as the leading edge of the modern departure from tradition, is at a crucial point of transition. Either it will be lost, assuming — with greater or lesser degrees of violence in the transition — the subservient position of an empire whose time has past, or it will become one of several societies, along with Australia, New Zealand, Bhutan, Brazil, Costa Rica, Germany, and the Netherlands, that lead the way in being not only post-traditional but also postmodern, as societies that are democratic and sustainable, societies in which material well-being is embraced and disciplined within a deeper and more broadly life-affirming sense of value. This is to say that it may not be too late, that people like Morris Berman who have concluded about America that "there is no warding off the Dark Age" may be speaking prematurely.[2] The positive alternative, which certainly exists in many of our hearts, in some relationships/communities in our nation, and in quite a few other places across the Earth, could be stronger than it appears.

This choice can be thought of on the analogy of the moment in the history of our species when prehistoric ancestors came to stand erect; when, unlike other animals, forelimbs ascended from the ground, allowing face and attention to rise upward, to live in a world of greatly expanded horizons. For the first time, humans were able to "lift mine eyes up unto the hills," withdrawing attention from the urgent immediacy of life on Earth to contemplate the mountaintops and the heavens, matters of value and meaning, within the kind of expanded consciousness which gave rise to the Axial Age foundation of the historic traditions.[3] The point is that our survival into the future depends on an analogous opening of horizons — most simply stated as an opening from short-term, individual interest to longer term, communal interests, and from regard for life on the planet as a trial to the capacity of a conscious mortal being to embrace life as a gift.

However, this dramatic image could be misleading, since emergence of a new worldview is *already going on in our midst*, though it is gradual, and a certain refocusing may be necessary to be able to see it. For Americans, focus must be adjusted to include the whole world, and to eliminate a certain distortion related to democracy and the mistaken assumption that it is a uniquely Western aspiration. Amartya Sen, champion of democracy as a commonly shared global heritage, attributes this distortion to "gross neglect of the intellectual history of non-Western societies."[4] Because of this distortion, America could fail to see the new worldview emerging in other parts of the world, or at home.

There are several circles of conversation through which the emergence of a new worldview is occurring quite visibly. These include the intercultural and interreligious dialogue movements, process philosophy, feminism, Third Epoch Confucianism, the environmental movement, higher education, postmodern philosophy, and American pragmatism. There is remarkable consistency among these conversations and the broader movement that together they carry. They all insist that our times require us to become conscious of the limitations of the worldview we inherit and to be responsible for the conscious task of choosing a more adequate worldview. They all point toward the emergence of a new worldview which is life-affirming, pluralistic, relational, ecologically responsible, and oriented to the transformation of all life in the direction of thriving. Some of these conversations point as well to the ways in which this "new" worldview also involves the re-valuing and re-appropriation of values that can be found in most of the world's traditions, including the American democratic tradition.

Consideration of "worldview" need not take us away from the world of politics and policy, as in so much of the "consciousness rising" activity of the past several decades. It is essential that the new worldview make it possible for us to live in the world with greater zest and joy, less ego inhibition, more responsiveness and appreciation, and greater compassion. It is a worldview of full presence, a worldview of ordinary human experience, of "return." Despite the fact that it needs interpretation to survive and grow, it is a worldview that is made manifest in acts of compassion rather than assent to doctrine. Awareness at the level of worldview can help us transition to a new worldview in which practice of civic virtue is discovered to be among the very best things we can do for *ourselves* as well for as others, through participation in the life-giving paradox of vital relationship. Healthy worldview can help us live more fully alive, at the same time it liberates us to care for/in the world. This applies to you and me in our local situations, and it also applies to the role of America and other nations in the larger world. To put the matter somewhat crudely, (re)discovery of the value of civic virtue can be seen as analogous to discovery of the need for regular physical exercise. It is an essential element of a good and healthy life.

But at some point the question arises: What can we say in more general terms about the nature of the new worldview? How can we support the many local emergences without insisting that they be either totally the same or completely different? This is not an easy question, especially if it is assumed that the "answer" must come in the form of a doctrine or a superior set of ideas, some grand and final abstraction to which all local instances must correspond, as was assumed historically within the dominant Western worldview. However, through the many embodiments and descriptions of the new worldview, identified more by their tone and consequences than their correspondence with creed, there are four points that are widely shared. First, ideas are relative to living, not the other way around; our lives cannot be either reduced to or derived from the ideas through/about which we speak. Rather, the quality of the life we live is either supported and enhanced by the ideas we adopt, or not. This implies that we have some perspective on the worldview we represent, as at least in part a limited human response to that which we and/or our ancestors perceive to be ultimate in life. In philosophical terms, this is to say we have achieved some degree of hermeneutical sophistication, understanding that human beings inevitably have an interpretation, though no one has *the* interpretation. All of us are in a life-long process of refining our interpretations. Second, the new worldview is, above all, *relational*. The purity of its presence is dependent on the quality of our relationships with others, the quality of our responsiveness, communication, and compassion. Further, the new worldview is *pluralistic,* reflective of *alterity* or otherness as a second root imperative and challenge of our era. Encounter with the Other requires maintaining a relationship that neither reduces the other to the same, nor pushes them to the incommensurable, living in the paradox of sameness and difference where human well-being occurs. This implies that we are able to affirm ongoing growth and refinement in relation to both the articulation and the practice of our worldview, along with others who are doing the same. The third point is affirmation of life, including the vast interdependence of the natural world within which life is given, in Hannah Arendt's words, as "a free gift from nowhere (secularly speaking)."[5] The new worldview entails movement beyond the Earth and the life-denying tendencies of both traditional and modern cultures, into a lifeway that values faithfulness to Earth as what William James calls "our common mother."[6] The fourth point is *development.* The new worldview that is emerging in our time both generates and depends on a maturity that was known at the foundation of the great traditions, but which has been largely eclipsed by both the oppressions of tradition and the distractions of the modern.

Dialogue is key in terms of how we can reappropriate traditional sources and preserve the best of modernity, in order to find a remedy for the modern condition. Dialogue indicates the essential relational dimension of a new worldview. Dialogue represents a new paradigm in which access to the spiritual power of the great traditions becomes surprisingly possible — the *power,* the sustaining energy, not just the ideas and colorful rituals. At the same time, it is also a way in which unity and diversity can be mutually supportive, breaking through the modern opposition between oppressive sameness on one side, and chaotic difference on the other. Diane Eck says it well: "Dialogue is premised not on unanimity, but on difference. Dialogue does not aim at consensus, but understanding. Dialogue does not create agreements, but it creates **relationships**."[7] For within and through dialogue, as the vibrant interplay between the similar and the different, and between the past and the present, we find a new home, a place of not only sustainability but also thriving, including the capacity to work with others on commonly shared problems with both self and world. Dialogue, then, in one sense *is* the new worldview. Yet some serious developmental work is required in order to get to this place.

ENDNOTES

1. William James, *The Varieties of Religious Experience* (London: Longman, Green, and Co., 1902), 53.

2. Morris Berman, *Dark Ages America: The Final Phase of Empire* (New York: Norton, 2006), 329.

3. Most recently on the significance of this shift in consciousness, see Karen Armstrong, *The Great Transformation: The Beginning of Our Religious Traditions* (New York: Knopf, 2006).

4. Amartya Sen, "Democracy and Its Global Roots," in *The New Republic*, 6 October 2003, 35.

5. Hannah Arendt, in her magnificent Prologue to *The Human Condition* (Chicago: University of Chicago Press, 1958), 3.

6. William James, *A Pluralistic Universe*, in *Essays in Radical Empiricism and a Pluralistic Universe*, ed. Richard J. Bernstein (New York: Dutton, 1971), 128.

7. Diana Eck, "Dialogue and the Echo Boom of Terror: Religious Women's Voices After 9/11," in Akbar Ahmed and Brian Forst, eds., *After Terror: Promoting Dialogue Among Civilizations* (Boston and Cambridge, UK: Polity Press, 2005), 28.

5

THE ADULTHOOD WE NEED

Education and Developmental Challenge in the U.S. and China

Surviving into the future requires that humans develop a maturity considerably beyond what has been accepted as "adulthood" in the past. This maturity is really no mystery. It has been well envisioned by both traditional cultures and, more recently, by social science, as well as by cultural movements such as pragmatism, process thought, and relational feminism.[1] Yet, strange as it may seem, cultivation of maturity has been largely ignored in the gold rush mentality of modern societies. More recently, liberal education—one of the world's great transformative practices—has even been scorned as "too expensive" in the midst of worldwide economic anxiety and the accompanying assumption that only technology and economic development will secure our future. Human wisdom, and a view of well-being that is both broader and deeper than the modern ideal of materialism, competition, and the Adam Smith doctrine of "automatic harmony," is rarely considered. But it is precisely *this* attitude that we can no longer afford, its shortsighted ignorance, shallow sense of value, and naïve assumption that somehow machines rather than human wisdom will solve our problems. We can no longer accept the marginalized status of non-STEM subjects such as those that constitute the humanities. Our job in higher education becomes one of the design and engagement of practices through which the human maturity we so urgently need can actually emerge and be present in the world. It is in this frame that we must argue for the humanities. My suggestion — and experience — is that this undertaking is most fruitful when we activate the resources of our respective traditions within a global project, which is to say, when we reappropriate our own practices for cultivation of mature human beings and engage with those from other cultures who are doing the same, within the framework of dialogue outlined in the previous chapter. Here is the fertile context in which we are able to draw most effectively on the riches of our separate pasts within a common present, in which the resources of other traditions can also become available to us, along with the considerable insights of social science and those movements I have mentioned. Here, for example, is where my own tradition of liberal education comes to radiant presence in our time. For whatever else maturity entails, it certainly must include the capacity to address commonly shared problems, such as the need for human beings who can thrive within a rich and endlessly challenging pluralistic environment.

I

With this thesis on the table, I would like to pick up from previous conversations with Chinese colleagues[2] and see if I can articulate some further direction for dialogue about the educational reform that is so crucial for the global future. I will do this by introducing three basic propositions, and then by offering suggestions as to response in our efforts to shape education for the global future.

PROPOSITIONS

First: modernity involves obsessive attention to the material conditions of existence, especially consumer satisfaction, and an intoxicated willingness to overlook or even sacrifice moral, spiritual, and cultural dimensions in the stampede toward the images of happiness presented by advertising, marketing, and the conspicuous consumption of celebrities. This overemphasis on what Martin Luther King, Jr. identifies as the external, physical, material dimension of human existence involves a neglect and depletion of basic human qualities associated with the internal, ethical, spiritual dimension,[3] a dimension that is utterly necessary to the development of wise and just policies for the deployment of technology and distribution of limited resources.

Second: The modern neglect of the distinctly human dimension is basic and potentially fatal from the perspective of all of the traditions from which modernity so energetically departed. Traditional cultures were aware that humans are different from other forms of life in that the mature or adult life does not simply unfold out of the natural process. An intervention into and modification, or enrichment, of the natural process must occur. In the Greek West this has been referred to as the cultivation of a "second nature," one that occurs through instruction and an explicitly transformative discipline. In the East, Xunzi's famous statement about heaven and human is analogous: "Heaven creates; humans complete." Neglect of cultivation or completion due to the distraction of modern consumerism is precisely the situation King spoke of as one of our having "guided missiles but misguided men."[4] Add the accelerating factors of technology and liberationist claims to equality in the modern rush, and there develops a veritable firestorm of distraction from this most fundamental traditional awareness about what it means to become fully human.

Third: The kind of intervention envisioned by the great traditions cannot occur by the simple technical or procedural means that are so familiar in our time. Another kind of action is required. There is a vast and decisive difference between "cultivating" and "constructing." In a technological era, it becomes difficult to see that the real education we seek cannot be training. The qualities we look for in the educated person cannot be imparted as performance skills, by breaking down complex actions into component steps. They cannot be transmitted as procedure, by reducing interactions to a finite list of functionally distinct types. From a Western perspective, education involves the mysterious doing of a thing "as an end in itself," or as something that is "good for its own sake," which is to say independent of results or attainment—even, paradoxically, of those most cherished human results we want to cultivate:[5] critical thinking, civic engagement, lifelong learning, and, perhaps at the very top of the list, *phronesis,* the practical wisdom that makes it possible for a human being to determine the right course of action in and through the particularity of life situations.[6] To look from just a slightly different angle, we can also say that education as cultivation of the adult human being inevitably involves encounter with what some have referred to as "the paradox of intention."[7] According to this paradox, in order to hit the mark, I must renounce my intention to hit the mark. This fundamental point helps us understand the inherent vexation of anything like genuine education—again, distinct from training—for technology and market-oriented societies.

II

Ours is a strange time indeed. For amidst gathering awareness of the threats and dangers of our era we come to see that what we so urgently lack in society today is precisely what was so clearly envisioned in the great or "Axial"[8] traditions of the past. If only we could reappropriate the wisdom our early modern ancestors so quickly dismissed as "old-fashioned" in the face of modern, material aspirations. But those traditional visions of human maturity and well-being (*eudemonia, xing fu,* what we are beginning in the global conversation to understand as "thriving" or "flourishing") were also mixed with values we now find completely unacceptable. The wisdom of tradition was intertwined with the racist, sexist, homophobic, and classist social forms that carried them. So "reappropriation of traditional wisdom" is no simple task.

I can speak most easily about the dynamics of reappropriation in relation to the Greek West. The Socratic wisdom, in its most compact and complete statement, envisions cultivation of the human through practice of "the examined life." Through repeated practice, gradually one's ego-driven ways of fear, ignorance, and desire give way to another kind of human being, one whose *daimon* shines through in reliably authentic presence.

But this understanding of the process of transformation was obscured and lost in the unfolding of Western history. First Plato interpreted the Socratic vision away from the relational practice that was integral to it into practices of learning arithmetic, plane geometry, solid geometry, etc., as successively higher orders of abstraction. Finally, in a degraded form of both the Socratic and the Platonic vision, and also the Aristotelian vision of cultivation through healthy habituation, assent to doctrine, or purely intellectual content, became the lens through which the Western canon of great works were to be "learned." Memorization and repetition became the pedagogy, as in any doctrinal orientation that values obedience and correctness of belief over any real human development. Here intellectual order triumphs over responsiveness to the complexities of embodied life. So along the way the Socratic practice was forgotten, and in the liberationist phase of early postmodernism, Socrates even came to be associated with the slavery, exclusion of women, and class stratification of Athenian society, and also with logocentrism, hegemonic universalizing, unsupportable meta-narratives, etc. The Socratic vision of a transformative practice was no longer available.

But today we are witnessing a breakdown of the old canon and questioning of education as transmission of doctrine. Cultural critique has moved from simple, critical theory deconstruction to something more sophisticated. With these, along with movement beyond postmodernist suspicion and reduction, we begin to enter an era in which we can speak again of a "virtues" or "capacities" orientation to education. Beyond a time when education was defined as rote learning of the canon, and beyond the ensuing postmodernism, when education was dominated by negative critique of that previous orientation, we are now entering an era in the West in which we can speak again of that deeper understanding of our heritage of liberal education as cultivation of beings who possess certain qualities that we recognize to be essentially human. From the perspective of "big history," this may be a really extraordinary moment in the unfolding of the human drama, as culture itself begins to become self-aware.

Something parallel might be occurring on the Chinese side. For we have come to see that in the roots of Chinese tradition there is a magnificent vision of human development.

Recall the discussion in Chapter Three about Chinese philosophy as *gong fu*. Its entire orientation is toward transformation, that great movement and accomplishment of *becoming human*. So those old scrolls and books never were intended as systematic philosophy, but represent collections of instruction and insight that were applied by a qualified master to particular students in particular times and places in relation to particular developmental challenges.

Liberating and inspiring as these insights are, however, they do not go very far in addressing the pedagogical issue of *how*. In a modern society dominated by an orthodoxy of number, technique, and cost-benefit-analysis, and given the absolutely critical distinction between education and training, how are we to actually engage the work of "completing and cultivating" the virtues that we can rather easily identify as the ones we desire.[9] In our day, many of us are pretty good on the *what* of education, but quite unclear about the *how*.

III

So it is that we suffer no want of vision in the matter of educating persons to be fully human, but rather a poverty of method—and some might say also of will, or of the ability to see the folly of giving up on the humanities as a necessary locus of the cultivation we advocate. The temptation to abandon the humanities to focus educational priorities strictly on STEM disciplines and implications for GDP is understandable, since this focus provides the illusion of satisfying scientific criteria and solving the method problem with quantifiable assessment instruments and outcome measures. It is easy to overlook the fact that this move involves the reduction and loss of vision. It becomes an ultimately fatal Faustian deal in which we choke off responsible citizenship, creative personhood, and the kind of innovation and discovery required for sustained economic—as well as civic and personal—well-being.

While I certainly do not have a complete answer to this most pressing challenge of method, I do want to make the case that it *is* our mutually shared global challenge; one we can far more effectively meet together as citizens of the same planet than we can in isolation. In this collaborative spirit, I offer some clues I am pursuing.

The first is to simply elaborate on the importance of a global and dialogical approach to education in order to release the efficacy and power of best local practices. Here is arguably the chief paradox of the 21st century: effective appropriation and engagement of local practices (e.g., Chinese, American, Vietnamese, Italian, etc.) requires that they be articulated in the global or universal context, and, conversely, that healthy and effective universalizations must remain rooted in local engagement. Another way to state this very basic and developmentally challenging paradox of our era is that, in order to insure and maintain the integrity of those practices that are particular to our own history and tradition, we must simultaneously adopt intercultural dialogue as an essential element of our pedagogy and practice, including even our *religious* practice. In this way we have access to an ever-present source of insight and critical awareness, help from others in the ongoing refinement of our living tradition, and appreciative perspective on the dignity and limitations of our own history and tradition. On the religious and/or spiritual point, we must be open to novelty, revelation, or discovery together, beyond all previous formulation. We must be open to encounter with the stranger who turns out to be a messenger of the divine.

Second, we need to draw on the impressive resources of social science that demonstrate a very strong correlation between cognitive development and the kind of moral and character development we seek to foster. Given this correlation and the specificity of capacities that are activated at each successive stage of human development, we can have a sense of which educational practices to engage and in what order. To take one of the most influential figures in this line of educational thinking as an example, Benjamin Bloom shows how we need to engage appropriate learning activities in order to facilitate development through six sequentially ordered domains of cognition: knowledge, comprehension, application, analysis, synthesis, and evaluation.[10]

Third, we need to reconsider some elements of traditional educational wisdom that may have been dismissed as "unscientific" from the perspective of modern enthusiasm for all things scientific. For example, there is the old Greek idea that a classic work is of value specifically by virtue of its *medicinal* value—as a *pharmacon*. A classical text cultivates character not through memorization of didactic assertion, but rather by a mysterious combination of example and mood, movement and outcome, and an ordering of words that can only be described as poetic. Its influence and benefit are in the act of reading itself. The similarity between this and the Chinese *gong fu* approach is obvious: reading great works *becomes* the practice. It is perhaps close to what Nussbaum is indicating by cultivation of "narrative imagination" in her short list of capacities or virtues.

Fourth, we need to respect modern wisdom, too. In fact, "reappropriation of traditional wisdom" that is not conducted in a dialogical relation with what is found to be positive in the modern moment seems inevitably to drift into some form of fundamentalist judgment, to some form of *jihad* against life in the present, and to more or less violent attempts to assert someone's simplified and idealized version of the past against the lostness of life in the modern present. The modern values of democracy, pluralism, and diversity; the integrity of individual experience; and the possibility of growth must not be dismissed in the midst of Western self-criticism.[11]

Here, from a Western perspective, I would cite the insights of John Dewey as a primary example of dialogue between tradition and modernity. He adapts the art of Socratic questioning into an inquiry-oriented pedagogy organized around the solving of problems and the framing and carrying out of purposes.[12] This approach, sometimes referred to as "active" or "progressive" learning, begins with the posing of problems or questions about which any functioning adult has at least some preliminary answer (e.g., What is good or true or beautiful?) and then proceeds to develop the views of students through conversational encounter with significant other figures who have agreed and disagreed with them in ways that help sharpen and deepen their own views. It is through this approach that Dewey and others have thought it possible for people to move beyond the strictly negative modern definition of freedom, which all too often prevails as merely "freedom from," to a positive understanding of freedom as the capacity to frame and execute purposes, thus moving toward what Marx articulated as the actualization of our ideal species nature with his central 1844 phrase, "free conscious activity."[13]

My fifth and last clue is most difficult to articulate. The cultivation we desire cannot be transmitted as doctrine through rote learning; it cannot be constructed as if we were assembling a machine; it cannot be reduced to a series of simple and repeatable actions, as in procedure. It is not an add-on or an accessory, but something we must *become* with our whole being, something like what used to be described as "soul," *ren* [full human-heartedness], or *cheng* [sincerity, reality].[14] Our aim must be the evocation (as in the original Western sense of education as *e-ducare,* to lead out or draw forth) of those key qualities of genuine adulthood, terms that are nearly squeezed out in the modern era, between mechanism/technology on one side, and criticisms of traditional religion/culture, (often associated with patriarchy, homophobia, and Earth/life denial), on the other.

Somehow education must not only teach students *about* this essential dimension of the person, it must *generate and nurture* that dimension as well. And as far as I can tell, the only way to do this is through the example and art of well-developed teachers. William James made this point very well over a century ago:

> you make a great, a very great mistake, if you think that psychology, being the science of the mind's laws, is something from which you can deduce definite programmes and schemes and methods of instruction for immediate classroom use. Psychology is a science, and teaching is an art; and sciences never generate arts directly out of themselves. An intermediary inventive mind must make the application, by using its originality.[15]

I cannot say exactly how it is done, this cultivation, this using the "originality" of an inventive mind—at least not in the scientific and "assessment" terms of our era. But I do know that some of the very best teachers, the ones who rise to the level of real and self-evident excellence, do so in virtue of a very essential and illusive quality and its infectious influence on their students.[16] From the perspective of embeddedness in our learning communities, we know it can be done— and we know, further, that a strongly international and dialogical orientation can generate a powerful synergy, as, for example, with the Chinese emphasis on human development through learning (*Xue*) alongside the Socratic commitment to identification and examination of basic values.

This is such a tall order. Perhaps I can be most helpful on this last and really most basic point about art and the necessity of embodiment by recommending three figures who are responsive to the issues I have mentioned above, and helpful as guides in the development we seek.[17] They each point to that synergy in which it actually becomes possible to cultivate or "complete" the genuine adult through bringing the missing dimension into education. They are Parker Palmer, Tu Weiming, and Martha Nussbaum.

Parker Palmer, beginning with his 1998 *The Courage to Teach,* has been extremely influential with teachers in America, helping us understand that excellent teaching comes not from application of technique, but through the identity and integrity of the teacher, echoing James' point about teaching as art rather than science. He continues to give encouragement and perspective to those who are deeply committed to the astonishingly unsupported teaching vocation in America, placing heart before technique, as the place in which intellect, spirit, and emotion converge. In his 2004 book, *A Hidden Wholeness,* he speaks of this convergence quite explicitly as *soul,* and teaching as a matter of "welcoming the soul," through creation of circles of trust, awareness of our parts in co-creating the world, and the power of our ongoing choosing of life.[18]

Second, Tu Weiming is one of the most distinguished public intellectuals and critics of that now global modern worldview that he calls "the Enlightenment mentality." He identifies the essential values of this now commonly shared legacy of the European Enlightenment as those of liberality, rationality, law, rights, and dignity of the individual, and shows how these values, held in abstraction from any other values, become radically problematic.[19] His recommendation as to the remedy is not that these now-global values be rejected, but that we broaden our intellectual scope and deepen our moral basis through a new paradigm of dialogue that enables us to integrate values excluded in the Enlightenment project, especially those of sympathy, relationality, and compassion.[20] He demonstrates how this can occur most effectively through dialogue with other traditions, especially Confucian humanism, as well as with feminism and the environmental movement.

Finally, Martha Nussbaum is also distinctly global in her scope and distinction, with roots in India as well as the U.S. She begins and ends the work she identifies as a manifesto, *Not For Profit: Why Democracy Needs The Humanities,* with the issue of soul.[21] She ends with the following:

> If the real clash of civilizations is, as I believe, a clash within the individual soul, as greed and narcissism contend against respect and love, all modern societies are rapidly losing the battle, as they feed the forces that lead to violence and dehumanization and fail to feed the forces that lead to cultures of equality and respect.[22]

Her remedy is to articulate a vision of healthy human development, with a corresponding pedagogy that supports people in the essential "struggle within each person, as compassion and respect contend against fear, greed, and narcissistic aggression."[23] Her aim is to cultivate precisely those capacities associated with the fully developed human being.[24]

IV

In each of these figures, a higher human capacity and an expanded sense of adulthood is associated with activation of a most fragile capacity called love or compassion, something that is very easy to dismiss as mere sentimentality. To cite a few other examples of those for whom the exercise of compassion is identified as the practice through which maturity emerges, Karen Armstrong, in her *The Great Transformation,* speaks of our need to "go in search of the lost heart, the spirit of compassion that lies at the core of all of our traditions."[25] Martin Luther King, Jr. speaks of our need for a "revolution of value" based on love as "that force which all of the great religions have seen as the supreme unifying principle of life," and "other preservation as the first law of life."[26] And Huston Smith concludes the later editions of the monumentally significant book he first published in 1958 as *The Religions of Man* with an appeal to listening to and understanding traditions other than our own. This is essential because "understanding brings respect, and respect prepares the way for a higher capacity which is love."[27]

But so much of education—and everything else in our era—is driven by technique and procedure, that these statements sound squishy or impossibly vague. They are far from the contemporary ideal of identification and execution of formal objectives that can then be assessed through quantifiable measures. In our time it is necessary to maintain awareness that those measures, which are so often presented with an air of self-evidency, are approximate at best, and that, at worst, they can perpetuate a dangerous illusion of order and control. Because they are necessarily based on reduction, from higher capacities to what are supposed to be the essential lower components of those capacities, these assessments actually stand on nothing more than the prevailing and ever-shifting managerial science of our day, and its unsupported assertions as to what constitute those relevant "lower components." It is as though the sheer complexity of it, along with certain legitimating association with "science"—plus the sometimes desperate and indiscriminate wish to have *something* by which to evaluate—serve to anesthetize people from seeing the flimsiness of these schemes. This same problem with contemporary assessment can also be described in terms of the relationship between metrics and goals, and the inevitable narrowness of any metric in the absence of clarity about goals. Carol Schneider, President of the Association of American Colleges and Universities, articulates this well:

> A high-quality accountability system to help determine the value of higher education needs to begin by clarifying the multiple important purposes of higher education—the educational goals—and not just with available measurement tools. Any single metric, by definition, is too narrow for the task of reporting multiple learning outcomes. Reporting "value" with a single metric is therefore potentially dangerous because the reporting itself marginalizes other equally important educational goals that the single tool was never intended to probe.[28]

"Clarifying the multiple important purposes of higher education" (or life) just may not be possible within the scientific paradigm, as we currently know it; in fact, this may be the defining flaw of that paradigm (or the dividing line between human and robotic behavior). Interdependent "multiple learning outcomes" may only be knowable in the realm of practical wisdom, only susceptible to reliable determination in the particulars of actual cases, only available to us as an art and not a science, through the master virtue of *phronesis* and what Kant calls "subjective universalization,"[29] which is to say, that source of truth and clarity that arises from the fully cultured attention to the depth of particularity.

Perhaps the most profound liability associated with the absence of this kind of discernment in our time is alienation from emergent truth. "Emergent truth" means discovery, possibility, novelty, growth; it means new energy entering the system. In the absence of emergent truth, entropy sets in, such that a gradual, often imperceptible downturn occurs. Growth, as anything more than quantitative increase or addition, is effectively prohibited, even met as a threat. In this atmosphere, there can be no increase in quality and no appeal to the common good. Notions associated with quality as anything beyond advertising or PR, as anything that goes to the core of the system—whether it be a university, a business, or an agency—will be identified as someone's attempt to advance their interest, and thereby relativized away. Such is the nihilistic game we so often play today.[30]

What could these considerations *mean* for life in the university today? All I have just said is very disturbing by the standards of science and its organizational arm, management. The quantitative orientation prevails, and is even accentuated through its frustration with occasional and partial awareness of the realities I discuss. Meanwhile the world waits for the emergence of a more sophisticated orientation to value, efficacy, and development; meanwhile the world waits for the adulthood we so urgently need.

For now, the mismatch between the relational event of real education and its intimate association with democratic community on the one hand, and the limitations of training and quantitative measure on the other, may well be a condition we need to live with as best we can, accepting that, in so many ways, we are living in an interim time. This awareness counsels modesty, creativity, flexibility, and an ever-deeper sensitivity to those educational dynamics through which the fully developed human being emerges. It is also worth pointing out that if we fail to live with some kind of grace in the mismatch between scientific rationality and humanistic cultivation, it will not likely be the romantic counterculture types, with their inability to distinguish between alternative methods and the abolition of method altogether, that we will need to worry about. Rather, the bigger threat will likely come from the well trained and undereducated managers who become fanatical in their impatience and their inordinate—though understandable—wish for order.

ENDNOTES

1   On these movements and their implications for our identification of adulthood, see my *Rediscovering the West: An Inquiry into Nothingness and Relatedness* (Albany: SUNY Press, 1994), especially chapter 9, "From Dialectic to Feminism." In *Overcoming America/America Overcoming: Can We Survive Modernity?* (Lanham: Lexington Press, 2012), I speak of "relational liberalism" as the genius of America which has been eclipsed by modernity, and which needs to be re-appropriated in dialogue with other societies which share a similar condition.

2   The present essay, though entirely independent, continues from earlier dialogues, such as one with Shanghai Jiao Tong University which is reported in *Soundings* as "Rediscovering Liberal Education in China: On the Benefits of Dialogue and Inquiry" (*Soundings* 96.2 (Fall 2013): 214–33.)

3   Martin Luther King, Jr., *Where Do We Go From Here: Chaos or Community?* (Boston: Beacon Press, 1967), 171.

4   King, 172.

5   The most influential articulation of the key capacities is that of the Association of American Colleges and Universities, in the form of the "Essential Learning Outcomes" of their Liberal Education and America's Promise (LEAP) program: "foundations and skills for lifelong learning, civic responsibility, integrative learning, critical thinking, intercultural knowledge and competence, and ethical reasoning." See: www.aacu.org/. Another influential list is that of Martha Nussbaum, in her *Not For Profit: Why Democracy Needs The Humanities* (Princeton: Princeton University Press, 2010): critical thinking, world citizenship, and narrative imagination.

6   *Phronesis,* as practical wisdom, is sometimes taken to be the practical equivalent to the more theoretical *Sophia* (wisdom), and is enormously significant insofar as it is beyond the dichotomies or antimonies we face today: between objective and subjective, absolute and relative, universality and particularity, etc. *Phronesis* points to a way of living and relating that is through and beyond the gridlock of our era. It is similar, as a developed capacity, to the Chinese *wu wei* (usually translated as action of non-action).

7   For an excellent comparative work on this important dynamic, see Marvin C. Shaw, *The Paradox of Intention: Reaching the Goal by Giving up the Attempt to Reach It* (Atlanta: Scholars Press, 1988).

8   This term, originated by Karl Jaspers in his 1953 *The Origin and Goal of History* (New Haven: Yale University Press, 1953), refers to the time in the first millennium BCE when the great traditions of the historical period emerged all across the Earth. Its dimensions and implications for life today are most recently articulated by Karen Armstrong in her *The Great Transformation: The Beginning of Our Religious Traditions* (New York: Alfred A. Knopf, 2006).

9   I have cited the recent AAC&U list of virtues or outcomes, as well as Martha Nussbaum's developed capacities. Here I would add a third list, one which emerged from consultation with Shanghai Jiao Tong University on the reform of Chinese general education: "cultivation of developed capacities for critical thinking, creative problem solving, and responsible innovation."

10 Benjamin Bloom, *Taxonomy of Educational Objectives: The Classification of Educational Goals* (New York McKay, 1956).

11 These key points about what is positive in modernity are easily

overlooked by those Western people who are driven by guilt over what their modern ancestors did, and the consequent need to "deconstruct." *See Overcoming America/America Overcoming,* 98.

12   It is interesting to note the influence of Dewey in China, and the compatibility of his progressive and pragmatic values with those of traditional China, before he was swept away by the arrival of Karl Marx. When I speak in China I often find myself in conversations that essentially involve the creativity of dialogue between Dewey and Marx. For the story of Dewey's presence in China, from May 3, 1919, through July 1921, see Jessica Ching-Sze Wang, *John Dewey in China: To Teach and to Learn* (Albany, NY: SUNY Press, 2007).

13   See: https://www.marxists.org/archive/marx/works/1844/manuscripts/labour.htm/.

14   On *Cheng* as the root virtue of Chinese civilization, see Yanming An, *The Idea of Cheng (Sincerity/Reality) in the History of Chinese Philosophy* (New York: Global Publications, 2005).

15   William James, "Psychology and the Teaching Art," in *Talks to Teachers on Psychology: and to Students on Some of Life's Ideals* (New York: Norton, 1958), 23–24.

16   See, for example, Joseph Axelrod, *The University Teacher as Artist* (San Francisco: Jossey-Bass, 1973). Perhaps this represents the kind of empirical approach to education we need. See also John K. Roth, ed., *Inspiring Teaching: Carnegie Professors of the Year Speak* (Bolton: Anker Publishing, 1997). I wonder how many of the teaching artists identified in these books would be identified by the instruments we use today.

17   This is consistent with the more empirical orientation to our questions I have already taken above, most recently with the Axelrod reference (n16). I take this turn to the empirical to be responsive to something William James said over a hundred years ago in one of his last lectures: "Let empiricism once become associated with religion [and he advocates and exemplifies the same association with education], as hitherto, through some strange misunderstanding, it has been associated with irreligion, and I believe that a new era of religion as well as philosophy will be ready to begin," in *Essays in Radical Empiricism and A Pluralistic Universe,* ed. Richard J. Bernstein (New York: Dutton, 1971), 270.

18 Parker J. Palmer, *The Courage to Teach: Exploring the Inner Landscape of a Teacher's Life* (San Francisco: Jossey-Bass Publishers, 1998), and *A Hidden Wholeness: The Journey Toward An Undivided Life* (San Francisco: Jossey-Bass, 2008).

19 Tu Weiming, "Beyond the Enlightenment Mentality," in *The Global Significance of Concrete Humanity* (New Delhi: Centre for Studies in Civilizations, 2010).

20 Weiming, "Beyond."

21 Nussbaum, *Not for Profit*, 6, 142.

22 Nussbaum, *Not for Profit*, 143.

23 Nussbaum, *Not for Profit*, 29.

24 See, most recently, Martha C. Nussbaum, *Creating Capabilities: The Human Development Approach* (Cambridge: Belknap Press, 2011).

25 Armstrong, *The Great Transformation*, 399.

26 King, *Where Do We Go From Here*, 190.

27 Huston Smith, *The Illustrated World's Religions* (San Francisco: Harper San Francisco, 1991), 249.

28 Carol Geary Schneider, "The Narrowing of the American Mind": http://chronicle.com/article/The-Narrowing-of-the-American/135212/, 2. I take this to be a radical statement, one with wide-ranging implications for all social assessment and policy formation, a statement which is in some ways analogous to Werner Heisenberg's "uncertainty principle" in physics.

29 Immanuel Kant, *Critique of Judgment*, Part I, Sections 6–9, especially Section 6. Also related to phronesis as the master virtue; see Karen Warren on "situated universality," in her *Ecofeminist Philosophy: A Western Perspective on What It Is and Why It Matters* (New York: Rowman and Littlefield, 2000), 113–15; and Tu Weiming on "the globalization of local knowledge," in "The Implications of the Rise of 'Confucian' East Asia," *Daedalus: Journal of the American Academy of Arts and Sciences* 129.1 (Winter 2000): 210.

30 See my *Overcoming Americ /America Overcoming*, chapter 3, "Moral Disease: The Late Modern Condition in America," 37–53.

6

ETHICS, TRANSFORMATION, AND PRACTICE

A Perspective on Liberal Education in the Global Age

I

INSOFAR AS LIBERAL EDUCATION is one of the world's great transformative practices, ethics is right at the heart of the matter — that is, insofar as we intend something more than mere training or socialization to established procedures; insofar as we still believe in the empowerment of the person as a reliable source of creativity and communal as well as individual well-being; insofar as we are serious about liberal education as the cultivated autonomy of persons who become capable of living "the examined life."[1]

From this perspective, ethics is the identification and cultivation of right and/or good action within a reciprocity that acknowledges both self and other, and sometimes in a relationality that recognizes obligation to others as the most effective way to engage the examined life. Examples are: "love thy neighbor as thyself" in Christianity, *Shu* (guiding one's action by taking the heart of the other as analogous to one's own) as method of *Ren* (full-hearted and mature personhood) in Confucianism, and Karen Armstrong's observation that *compassion* was the central religious practice of all of the great traditions in the Axial Age.[2]

This definition of ethics as a matter of how we live within the self-other tension implies that how we are living now is not quite right. Ethics in any robust sense contains both theoretical and practical dimensions; both 1)"identification," in some kind of language or art, of right action, and 2) "cultivation," as the attempt to internalize and manifest this rightness so that it occurs with ever greater frequency in our lives. Theory without practice becomes an unexamined practice in itself, which is undisciplined by consequences or what is actually going on in the world; practice without theory is either *ad hoc* or submission to someone else's understanding of the good. Understanding and action are ineluctably reciprocal in human life. They constitute a delicate balance that can be broken or distorted in many ways.

Ethics, then, is among the highest of human arts and a major repository of our deepest aspirations. And for this very reason it can go terribly wrong. Because of its reach—from what we presently are to what we need to become—ethics is always becoming confused with something else. The most common confusion is identification of ethics with either relativistic personal preference or mere obedience to authority, whether it be that of religion, science, or managerial procedure. In our era, despite superficial freedoms, the danger of these confusions is very strong, especially as the arts in general are little recognized as anything other than their reduced value as commodity or decoration.

In the midst of this condition, the question of how ethics should be "taught" in an educational setting (higher, lower, or in between) is challenging indeed. The purpose of this essay is to clarify some of the main challenges and then to move on to consideration as to how ethics might best be identified and cultivated in the context of an undergraduate, baccalaureate curriculum, which maintains some connection with the historic aims of liberal education.

II

First the challenges.

In the not-so-distant past, ethics was owned by philosophy departments and, sometimes, by religion, or public relations departments. But then, in a time that roughly corresponds with the emergence of the postmodern critique of traditional Western culture, it was discovered that ethics as taught in most philosophy departments had serious problems. It labored under the structuralist assumption of a displaced and static metaphysical reality that could be known by humans in a one, best theory. This led to arguments, which became absurd, between philosophers as to whose one, best theory was actually *the* one, best one.[3] This left many to laugh at and dismiss philosophers, because common sense told them quite well that the competing theories are actually alternative insights on the matter of right/good action. Maybe philosophers couldn't handle the complexity and ambiguity of real life, but any ethically sensitive person—and anyone who cares more about other persons than they do about their own theoretical correctness—knows that we must live with a degree of uncertainty, as well as appropriate modesty about what we can know. Socrates' confession that he knows nothing remains good, if somewhat mysterious, advice.

But something a little more severe than laughter and dismissal emerged with the postmodernist unveiling of a deeper problem with traditional Western philosophical ethics. Philosophical ethics was discovered to be radically insensitive to both persons and life situations in its urge to turn away from life in order to find out what was called for by theory. In other words, the philosophical approach, when confronted with a situation in which the question of good/right action arose, would not look deeply into the situation itself to discover the complexities and imperatives that are implicit therein. Rather, the philosopher wanted to abstract immediately; first, by identifying the "maxim," or ethically relevant situation; and second, by rushing to theory in order to hold the maxim up to the established rules. Only then would the philosopher return to the scene of action and relationship with the "right" answer. This orientation was discovered to be arrogant, involving the very hegemonic and false universalizing that liberation movements were uncovering as the Western colonial attitude. It was also narrowly logocentric, or intolerably immature.[4]

These revelations led those committed to liberal education and its intimate connection with ethics either to look outside of philosophy departments, or to take matters into their own hands. By the mid-70s, "ethics," as an academic subject, was beginning to appear "across the curriculum," especially in professionally oriented programs. There it became either a component of existing courses or was offered as a freestanding course. But with proliferation, new challenges began to appear. Too often professional faculty, teaching most often with a case and inquiry method, lacked the philosophical sophistication to bring ethical implications fully to light or to guide inquiry. Too often, students learned little more than the relativity of ethics, and perhaps some diplomatic skills in navigating sensitive ethical territory. Or worse, they learned the traditional situation-insensitive form of ethics, now through the strategic plans of management science, with mission, goals, and values applied downward to objectives and measurable behaviors, essentially replacing ethics with procedures.

In general, then, efforts to teach ethics in recent decades have demonstrated the deep Western tendency to dichotomize theory and practice. The tendency was for thinkers to drift to one side of the room, creating theories abstracted from real life; and for actors to drift to the other side of the room, where they mindlessly applied whatever procedures or preferences were in force. Responding to this and other challenges, and to bring this very brief story of ethics in the university in recent times to the present, a group emerged to think about issues, empower teachers, and advocate for ethics across the curriculum—the Society for Ethics Across the Curriculum.[5]

III

Components of a new course:

With all of the above as background, and returning to the original concern with liberal education, ethics, and practice, I would now like to offer a suggestion about the design and pedagogy of ethics courses in an undergraduate curriculum. This I will present "snowball style," which is to say, starting with core commitments and then "rolling" in other components that can adhere to the original and developing body of suggestion. There are six core commitments.

First, an adequate ethics course needs to be oriented to transformation, or, as we more likely say today, to development. It needs to engage practices that have the effect of supporting and strengthening ethical development, helping the student to become more alert and responsive in life situations that are ethically sensitive. For what the world needs so urgently is not, after all, more rules, procedures, and competing ideologies, but more ethically developed human beings.[6]

It is important to note here that much of the discussion of ethics in the 20th century and beyond, beginning with the work of Piaget and American pragmatists William James, Jane Addams, and John Dewey, has been focused on development, with Benjamin Bloom, Lawrence Kohlberg, Carol Gilligan, William Perry, and Martha Nussbaum being the primary voices in higher education. While there is no easy unanimity among these figures as to what constitutes healthy development, a strong pattern emerges, one in which ethical development is closely linked to cognitive development, along the lines indicated by Bloom in 1956.[7] From the developmental perspective, exercise of the "ethical muscle" should be a major component of an ethics course. This is the muscle of reflection or reflexivity[8] within the self, and deliberation with others, regarding ethical significance and action.

This leads to the case/situation approach. A second component of an ethics course would be analyzing situations or cases to identify the ethical issues contained within them. It involves becoming aware of the full array of positions one might take, engaging in deliberation with others who represent at least some of these alternative positions, and taking a stand as to right or good action. Here we engage the actual practice. In this, it is important to consider whether one can come to agreement on what is good or right with persons who take positions that are different from one's own. It is also important to keep in mind the above process of moving from case to decision, so that this process can be revisited and evaluated later in the course.

A third component would be inquiry. This is to say that discussions of ethical development and cases are embedded within an ongoing adventure of the class in relation to the most general problematic: What is good or right action, and how is this to be determined in the situational immediacy of real life? As a class proceeds, certain themes and positions will emerge from the uniqueness of the students present in the class, ones that cannot be anticipated in the professor's prior construction of the syllabus. It is essential for the class and the professor to 1) identify those emergent themes and positions as they appear, 2) bring resources to their investigation and evaluation (perhaps bringing in more specialized information related to the professions or legislative processes necessary for a full understanding of the situation), and 3) weave ongoing discussion of them into subsequent meetings of the class. This means that the course must be structured in a syllabus that is both definite about material and practices—dates for exams/papers and transition points between parts of the course—and at the same time open to an emergent design that can embrace and pursue discovery. Needless to say, this requires a teacher who is skilled not only in the cognitive content of the course, but one who is also excellent in the art of inquiry, deliberation, and ethics itself.

A fourth element would be examination of the broadest possible array of positions, perspectives, or ideological commitments people take in relation to ethics. Here is where the content of traditional philosophy courses comes into play. As above, however, I recommend that material on position and perspective not be taught on the presumption that one must be right and all others wrong. Moreover, having a position should not exempt one from serious attention to a situation wherein determination of good or right is simply a matter of application. In a course that is adequate to our global environment, and perhaps also to a higher order of expectation and advancement with respect to ethical development, it is essential to maintain a certain reverence for the concrete immediacy of lived life and the unique situations that constantly flow from it. And we might add that a corollary of this reverence—yes, a term with religious connotation—is honoring the fact that in at least some cases there is a mysterious way in which good or right action in that situation is self-evident.[9]

Note, however, that here is where the skill of the teacher again becomes crucial. The fact that there is no traditional, metaphysically supported, one right answer to an ethical question (except in the minds of ideologues in the room[10]) need not mean that we have hit the slippery slope that descends directly into the quagmire of relativism. It seems especially important for students today to confront directly this either-or, the dilemma or "Catch 22," between absolutism and relativism. It seems also necessary that they experience the initially disturbing sense in which one theoretical position might be most telling in one situation, and a different position in the next. For example, sometimes consequences (or a teleological perspective) are decisive. Other times the (deontological) state of the actor's intention is most significant. What the world needs is neither more sophisticated (and often more nihilistic) relativists, nor more shrill ideologues, but more developed human beings who are equipped with a strong awareness of the full range of ethical positions. These include the affirmations contained in most of them, as well as their typical liabilities; that is, there are far fewer perverse positions than most people think, and problems arise when we attempt to affirm one thing (like individuality) so strongly that we develop a blind spot for other values (like community) to the point of destructive distortion and ultimately self-contradiction.

This leads to a fifth component: the recognition and cultivation of dialogue (or deliberation, or democratic citizenship) as the central ethical art. Here the dialogue among civilizations that is occurring in our time can be especially helpful.[11] This entails encounter with the other who is different, in the kind of interaction in which differences can be refined and enhanced at the same time that we are able to work together on real problems and issues more effectively than before. As Diana Eck put it, "the purpose of dialogue is not agreement, but relationship."[12]

For example, dialogue with Chinese Confucian colleagues can be very helpful as to the informing vision of another very significant part of the world. It can also be very informing of *our part* of the world, bringing deeper insight to the commitments we already hold. Returning to examples cited at the beginning of this essay, awareness of Confucian *shu* (or the Chinese negative golden rule of not doing to others what you wouldn't want done to yourself) as the practice through which we can become fully human illuminates "love thy neighbor as thyself" not as commandment but as advice and identification of where life is vital and real.

There is one final component that I would like to suggest, and it is one that takes us back to reverence. I think it is essential to a complete and effective ethics course that it present heroes. By this I mean letting students see inspiriting examples of humans rising above impossible constraints and temptations to do the right thing. A good source here would be Philip Hallie's study of the people of Le Chambon, a small village in the Swiss Alps that saved many Jews during the Nazi era at great risk to themselves, a place, in Hallie's beautiful phrase, "where goodness occurred."[13] Other examples might come from the lives of students and raise the question as to the distinction between true heroism and celebrity.

Presentation of heroes is a way to give students a glimpse of the higher rungs of ethical development, the most mature orientation, indicated by the Greek *phronesis,* the practical wisdom of judgment in the particulars of the situation, without dependence on external rules; or the Indian *upaya,* the skillful means and sense of appropriateness, which is, again, situation-based; or the Chinese *wu wei,* the action of non-action, which corresponds with Confucius' description of the highest ethical stage of development as the time when one is finally able to "follow my heart's desire without ever transgressing the way"[14]—or, in the more contemporary terms of Robert Pirsig's *Zen and the Art of Motorcycle Maintenance,* to act out of "the silence that allows you to do each thing just right."[15]

IV

Teaching ethics means teaching—and, again, both identifying and cultivating—confidence in human beings, and along with this, awareness that there are decisions upon which the future of the human race and indeed all life on this planet depend, decisions that cannot be made by machines. Teaching this confidence requires that students revisit the old Western idea of *conscience,* and with it entertain the possibility that all healthy human beings have the capacity to judge right from wrong—again, beyond cynical reductions of ethics to matters of power, preference, conditioning, and genetics. It is time for humans to learn to live and thrive in the complexity, ambiguity, and incompleteness of the world as it is, and in so doing learn also to live with greater compassion and appreciation.[16]

This is to suggest that ethics needs to be taught in context, specifically the context of both the actual lives that students are living today and also the broader context of technological determinism and commodification, which together can make ethics as anything other than the Ayn Rand "objectivism" of pursuing self-interest seem naïve. This is to say that an effective ethics course cannot be taught in a cloister. Students need to study ethics while having a guided confrontation with the facts of life in our time and on our planet, as the only honest groundwork upon which to enter a life in which the consideration, refinement, and choice of ethical commitments can be possible.

ENDNOTES

1. Plato, *Apology* 38a, in *The Collected Dialogues of Plato,* eds. Edith Hamilton and Huntington Cairne, Bollingen Series, no. 71 (New York: Pantheon Books, 1985), 23.

2. Karen Armstrong, *The Great Transformation: The Beginning of Our Religious Traditions* (New York: Alfred A. Knopf, 2006), 399.

3. On this theme, see Mary Midgley, "Sustainability and Moral Pluralism," in Victoria Davion, ed., *Ethics and the Environment* (Greenwich, CT: JAI Press, 1996), 41–54.

4. For an expanded treatment of these themes, see my *Overcoming America/America Overcoming: Can We Survive Modernity?* (Lanham, MD: Lexington Books, 2012).

5. See: www.seac.org/. See also the Society for Values in Higher Education at www.SVHE.org, and the Association of American Colleges and Universities at www.aacu.com, especially its LEAP Program, "Liberal Education and America's Promise," as two other associations that are responsive to these concerns.

6. On the need for a mature or more fully developed form of humanity, see my *Overcoming America / America Overcoming*.

7. Benjamin Bloom, *Taxonomy of Educational Objectives: The Classification of Educational Goals* (New York: McKay, 1956).

8. On the need for reflexivity, see Alison Jaggar's classic essay, "Love and Emotion in Feminist Epistemology," in *Inquiry* 32.2 (1989): 151–76.

9. For a classic reflection on this self-evidency, see Joseph Fletcher, *Situation Ethics: The New Morality* (Louisville: Westminster John Knox Press, 1966).

10. The best single short work I know of on the cultural and political

dynamics of ideology is Hannah Arendt, "Ideology and Terror: A Novel Form of Government," in *The Origins of Totalitarianism* (Cleveland and New York: Meridian Books, 1958), 460–79. See also Richard Bernstein, *The Abuse of Evil: The Corruption of Politics and Religion since 9/11* (Cambridge, UK, and Malden, MA: Polity Press, 2005). In contrast to the ideological orientation, Bernstein discusses fallibalism and the significance of epistemic pluralism.

11 For a discussion of dialogue in relation to development, see my "Dialogue, Development, and Pluralism," in *Overcoming America/America Overcoming*, 115–26.

12 Diana Eck, "Dialogue and the Echo Boom of Terror: Religious Women's Voices After 9/11," in Akbar Ahmed and Brian Forst eds. *After Terror: Promoting Dialogue Among Civilizations* (Cambridge, UK, and Malden, MA: Polity Press, 2005), 28.

13 Philip Hallie, *Lest Innocent Blood Be Shed* (New York: Harper & Row, 1979), reflecting the more empirical approach to ethics I am recommending.

14 Confucius, *Analects* 2:4, in *The Analects of Confucius,* trans. Roger T. Ames and Henry Rosemont, Jr. (New York: Ballantine, 1998), 76–77.

15 Robert Pirsig, *Zen and the Art of Motorcycle Maintenance* (New York: William Morrow, 1974), 242.

16 On the urgent need for an expanded adulthood that embraces these and other key capacities, see my "The Adulthood We Need: Education and Developmental Challenge in the U.S. and China," in Judy Whipps, ed., *Reflect, Connect, Engage: Liberal Education at Grand Valley State University* (Acton, MA: XanEdu Custom Publishing, 2013).

7

ON COMMITMENT AND CIVILITY

And Why the One Requires the Other

MICHAEL BLOOMBERG, AT RECENT HARVARD GRADUATION ceremonies, compared what he sees as the current liberal exclusion of conservatives in American higher education to 1950s McCarthy-era persecution of liberals by conservatives. But what is "liberal" and what is "conservative"? And who is excluding and being excluded in the present? I think there is a deeper distinction we need to be aware of in order to take on these important questions with any effectiveness.

The students and faculty who rejected graduation speakers at Brandeis, Rutgers, Smith, and other universities—including Harvard protests against Bloomberg for his "stop and frisk" policies—need to be understood, as Bloomberg himself suggested later in his speech, not only in terms of the content of the policies they advocate or reject, but also in terms of their affirmation of toleration. But to think that this essential quality of toleration is a property of either liberals or conservatives is a grave mistake.

The terms "liberal" and "conservative" quickly begin to slide around and become incoherent if they are taken to indicate a fixed set of politically correct positions on particular issues. "Liberal" cannot mean neoliberal absolutized faith in market capitalism, or reduction of all relationships to rights and contracts. And neither can "conservative" be equated with absolute defense of the individual, minimal government, or the Tea Party demands that have so damaged the Republican Party. Rather, both terms indicate a complex life-disposition. Both are obscured and co-opted in the absence of their deep agreement about tolerance and free inquiry that has enabled them — one more forward-looking and confident in the human capacity to create a better life, the other more likely to find wisdom and guidance in the past — to coexist and provide a more or less healthy tension as the medium of public life in the West. Liberals have needed conservatives to save them from hubris and remind them of the importance of foundation; conservatives have needed liberals to prevent them from becoming stodgy and closed-off to discovery. Like dynamic and form, these two great principles have enjoyed symbiosis and even synergy in the part of our history that is great and worth saving.

The deep agreement that has been shared by these historic dispositions is the value, some would even say the *sacred* value, of public discourse, where each party comes to the table with a position but also a willingness to listen to others with whom they initially disagree. They come in the maturity of knowing that their position is not necessarily *the* one, best position. They come with a willingness to be persuaded through the reasonableness of the other. And they come with a certain belief that a larger truth, or at least a solution to the immediate problem, might be revealed when they meet and relate in this way.

In the contemporary American university, this deep agreement is eclipsed by two of the chief qualities of culture in our time. The first is cultural critique, which is to say, awareness and critical assessment of the underlying assumptions of the culture that had functioned unconsciously in the past. Most of it is negative deconstruction, an unmasking and tearing down of the values and institutions that had dominated before. Critique becomes ambiguous because, while it serves to liberate in a further extension of the modern project of individual freedom and breaking down barriers to inclusion, it also breeds an atmosphere of competition and suspicion, resulting in inability to trust or sustain belief in the possibility of discovery or disclosure of the truth through interaction with those with whom we disagree. In its more intense forms, critique generates forms of critical theory that become nihilist, reducing everything to a function of interest and power; ironically, the very "war of all against all" the early modern theorists were seeking to escape. And at its outer edges, cultural critique can generate fundamentalist reaction, and even terrorism. It is in relation to these phenomena that some recent studies observed that American higher education is imbalanced in emphasizing critique to the exclusion of appreciation.

A second expression of cultural instability that is of particular concern in higher education today is polarization, variously referred to as "Catch 22," "double bind," dilemma, and either-or. Whatever cultural-relational magic (or hegemony) held things together in the past has eroded away, and we find ourselves standing on the edges of a field of endless opposition. This situation, one tat is arguably inherent in the antagonistic logic of modernity, is perhaps especially difficult for Western people, because our historic preference for intellectual solutions and doctrine inclines us to ideological rigidity in the post-traditional and postmodern present. So we suffer, along with society in general, the gridlock of ideological standoff.

The contemporary university, then, is more complex than Bloomberg's first remarks imply. In the stress and constriction of our era we have intolerance and ideological assertion from several quarters, including some, like the managerial mindset infecting American higher education in this time, that are not even "political" in the usual senses of that term. The real distinction we need to make is between absolutists, those who insist that all must accede to the correctness of their position, whether they be on the right or the left, and those, on the other hand, who are both willing and able to engage that essential human capacity that is variously called dialogue, inquiry, deliberation, or substantive democracy (as distinct from its merely procedural form).

The deep and fundamentally educational problem of our time is that the essential capacity to which I appeal is a *developed* capacity, and precisely one that has been eroded by the hyper-critical and even self-punishing character of American culture in recent decades. We've seen this before in American history: times when dangerous dynamics (e.g., exceptionalism, world wars, economic crisis, Cold War) frightened the more generous and mature side of American culture into regression, causing the country's withdrawal from its more sincere engagement with the world into absolutized pillbox-like positions.

I know of only one way to encourage the toleration and free inquiry we so urgently need. It arises from the utterly crucial developmental moment when we come to realize that critique alone is not sufficient. At that point we need to resist the sometimes subtle temptation of various forms of ideological rigidity and/or fundamentalism (some of them secular, such as those associated with market economics or the forms of critical theory mentioned above). We need to push past critique alone to identify our positive reason for being in the world, our contribution, our *commitment*. One aspect of this most basic movement of "return" is that it requires us to consciously engage the task (in German, *aufgabe,* task as obligation) of reappropriating the best in our past and tradition, while leaving behind those qualities that are problematic (racism, sexism, classism, etc). Further, we need to understand that the crucial realization, and the process of reappropriation that follows from it, happens most effectively in the company of others who are not the same. They are different from us, but engaged in the same task of sorting out what is best in both their traditions and also in modernity. Again, this must become a conscious act. As the great, late sociologist Robert N. Bellah has pointed out by way of saying what is so radically different about our era, culture must now become self-aware. We must each become responsible for our choice of symbol system, and thereby conscious agents of an emerging global culture that is both one and many.

Taking up this task both consciously and in the presence of others who are and remain different—even as the commonality of friendship grows—makes it possible for us not only to reappropriate the best of our own traditional past, but also to have access to the wisdom of other traditions. We develop that deep commonality that can stabilize polarization and transform difference into a source of vitality.

Much of the internal tension in the university between various faculty and administrative groups would evaporate if we could focus in this mode on our commitment to students—as human beings, not just as consumers or future functionaries. Our focus should be on helping them undergo the developmental movement described above, maturing into the capacity for dialogue on the unsteady ground of the present. One way to speak about what this entails is in terms of the widely influential William Perry paradigm, from his *Forms of Moral and Intellectual Development in the College Years* (1968).[1] He speaks of a deep curriculum of educational-personal development that occurs in a college education when things go right: from traditional absolutism to post-traditional relativism, and then from relativism to "commitment," as the mature stage in which one becomes capable of choice and definiteness in the midst of uncertainty and flux. But in the 21st century—in light of polarization, gridlock, and the "politicization" of everything—we need to go beyond Perry to distinguish between healthy and unhealthy forms of commitment. We need to cultivate the arts of dialogue and "free inquiry" as the media through which healthy commitment develops and continues to grow. For healthy commitment cannot mean taking up residence within a closed ideology. Healthy commitment exhibits a paradoxical simultaneity between the definiteness of taking a stand and openness to the other and new insight.

This capacity for a kind of commitment that is at one with civility is predicated on two fairly simple (not to say easy) qualities. The first is the hermeneutical sophistication of realizing that my commitment and the stand I take is limited, an expression of my time and place and personality, and all the many other contingent factors that constitute my life. I come to realize that, while universalizing is a natural human phenomenon, I am in no position to legislate to others in any but persuasive senses the universalizations I create or choose—apart from the affirmation of toleration and free inquiry. This, of course, is mind-boggling from the standpoint of our ancestors: that we can take a position and universalize it without absolutizing it—and all within a context of civility that is now global rather than tribal.

The second capacity is that of growth. Once I am liberated from needing the assurance that my position is aligned with the absolutely superior position, I can affirm the radical ineffability of that which is ultimate in life. I can then enjoy a pluralism that is quite distinct from the "whatever" invocation of relativism, and that is the ongoing growth that occurs through the presence of others who are different. I am liberated to discover with those others that we participate in the sacred space of encounter, where the Ultimate often is manifest more intensely than in either privacy or sameness.

My point is that to focus on our commitment to students and their development as human beings, as the center of a liberal education, is the most effective way to address our problems with polarization and reappropriate our own civility. Our universities and our faculties should model the very same maturity we seek to cultivate in our students. If we can model a better world, and send graduates out there who embody a new vision of unity in diversity, we might even make a difference in unlocking the power of America and other societies to do real and substantial good. In fact, there is already some evidence that this is happening.

ENDNOTES

1   William Perry paradigm, from his *Forms of Moral and Intellectual Development in the College Years* (New York: Holt, Rinehart, nd Winston, 1968.)

Part TWO

Broader Horizons

8

LIBERAL EDUCATION

Cornerstone of Democracy

IF WE WANT AN EGALITARIAN DEMOCRACY, we must prepare for it and create it by providing the prerequisite conditions. One of those conditions is widespread involvement in interactive or participatory processes that constitute public dialogue. The aim of that involvement is to build the capacity in ourselves and our fellow citizens for a relational understanding of the world—one in which each of us is engaging in committed action, not simply observing as bystanders or acquiring as consumers. In this essay, I will argue that liberal education is one of the most important, and often overlooked, forms of democratic practice. It is, therefore, an essential prerequisite for the continuation and expansion of democracy.

There are types of democracy that do not presuppose the active involvement of all citizens. Democracy as it was first practiced in ancient Athens emerged in a slave-owning society. The first eight decades of constitutional democracy in the United States also left the question of slavery up to each state. "Elite democracy" may sound like an oxymoron, and yet that has been the primary form of this institution until now. The sort of democracy in which ordinary

---

This article appeared previously in *American Journal of Economics and Sociology* 76.3 (May 2017): 579–617.

citizens would have a high degree of social equality and develop institutions for self-governance has remained more of an aspiration than a reality.

This essay addresses what we might call "true democracy" or "egalitarian democracy"; a system of self-governance that demands a great deal of citizens and that aspires to treat all citizens with justice and fairness. This is a far cry from the system of constitutional democracy that embraces the rule of law and formal procedures, but allows institutions that deny the majority of citizens genuine involvement in the decisions that shape public life to prevail. It also goes far beyond the many forms of democracy in the world today in which citizenship consists of little more than choosing between political parties on voting day. To achieve a full-fledged democracy requires active efforts to bring about the conditions that make it possible. That is a task requiring commitments from a wide range of citizens.

A highly skewed distribution of wealth and ownership of productive enterprise is an obstacle to true democracy, because it creates a condition of economic dependence in the population that undermines the capacity for self-governance. For that reason, Thomas Jefferson proposed that every adult receive 50 acres of land:

> Every person of full age neither owning nor having owned 50 acres of land, shall be entitled to an appropriation of 50 acres or to so much as shall make up what he owns or has owned 50 acres in full and absolute dominion. And no other person shall be capable of taking an appropriation.[1]

Jefferson's aim was to create a system of property in which no person was beholden to another for a livelihood, since he held that a loss of economic autonomy would prevent democracy from flourishing. According to Jefferson: "Dependence begets subservience and venality, suffocates the germ of virtue, and prepares fit tools for the designs of ambition."[2] This was an early statement of the material basis of democracy.

If the fruits of toil are shared sufficiently to enable every citizen to participate in public life with some degree of effectiveness, that is a necessary condition for true democracy, but not a sufficient basis for it. As Jefferson and the other founders of the United States understood, a self-governing nation, in which sovereignty lies with the people rather than an aristocracy, must provide the means to cultivate citizens who are not only productive but who also share a vision about the common good. To achieve that requires educational institutions designed to fulfill that purpose.

THE PECULIAR ROLE OF LIBERAL EDUCATION IN DEMOCRACY

Liberal education is an essential element in the development and perpetuation of democracy. The contribution of liberal education to democracy operates independently of the economic and social basis of democratic life. We shall return below to the precise nature of liberal education, but, for the moment, we must first ask what function it serves.

Liberal education is not only *preparation* for democracy, it *is* democracy. This is a striking notion, at odds with our usual instrumental view of "civics" education and other elements of the curriculum that are designed to teach citizens the formal structures of democratic process. The idea that liberal education is itself constitutive of democracy goes far beyond that simplistic view.

The relationship of liberal education to democracy is undoubtedly hard to discern if one's familiarity with higher education is limited to the factory-like atmosphere in some modern universities. Although most universities have a "college of arts and sciences," and some even have a "college of liberal arts," the bureaucratic management of the modern university is, in many ways, the antithesis of democracy.

There are several characteristics of liberal education that lie at the heart of democracy, and each is also a precondition of human maturity:

- Mutual engagement in relation to the issues of public or common life;
- Pursuit of the ability to state one's own position and at the same time be open to the positions of others;
- An openness to new or expanded truth that emerges from dialogical encounter;
- A community in which diversity and unity are mutually enhancing; and
- Continuous learning, growth, and good policy decisions.

Note that these elements are not contingent on any particular curriculum or institutional structure. In my view, liberal education consists of learning that is oriented toward a set of attitudes and human relationships that cultivate or develop both personal integrity and social integration.

Many things, of course, are labeled "liberal education," since the term itself, like "democracy" or "dialogue," carries a favorable connotation. But this label is inappropriate unless the educational form to which it is affixed shows substantial commitment to the core practice of open inquiry in a dialogical community. There is no specific content to liberal education, such as the great books of Western civilization, or any other form of accumulated knowledge. What matters ultimately is an approach to knowledge that presupposes its connection to lived experience.

Without this core practice of critical appropriation of past knowledge, combined with appreciation of its ongoing significance, education becomes mere transmission of what Whitehead calls "inert knowledge,"[3] or what James referred to as "reception without reaction" and "impression without correlative expression."[4] Dewey also found most modern education failing the test of liberal education, referring to the alternative as "the beauty parlor" conception of art and ideas.[5]

Paolo Freire has more recently compared: 1) "the banking concept" of education, in which knowledge is deposited into passive students, to 2) "problem-posing" education, in which teachers facilitate learning by posing questions related to experience:

> In the banking concept of education, knowledge is a gift bestowed by those who consider themselves knowledgeable upon those whom they consider to know nothing.... The teacher talks about reality as if it were motionless, static, compartmentalized, and predictable. Or else he expounds on a topic completely alien to the existential experience of the students. His task is to "fill" the students with the contents of his narration—contents that are detached from reality, disconnected from the totality that engendered them and could give them significance. Words are emptied of their concreteness and become a hollow, alienated, and alienating verbosity...
>
> In problem-posing education, people develop their power to perceive critically the way they exist in the world with which and in which they find themselves; they come to see the world not as a static reality, but as a reality in process, in transformation... Hence, the teacher-student and the students-teachers reflect simultaneously on themselves and the world without dichotomizing this reflection from action, and thus establish an authentic form of thought and action.
>
> Banking education resists dialogue; problem-posing education regards dialogue as indispensable to the act of cognition which unveils reality. Banking education treats students as objects of assistance; problem-posing education makes them critical thinkers. Banking education inhibits creativity... thereby denying people their ontological and historical vocation of becoming more fully human. Problem-posing education bases itself on creativity and stimulates true reflection and action upon reality.[6]

Freire applied his principles to adult education in poor barrios in Brazil, where he demonstrated that problem-posing education has the potential to catalyze revolutionary change. In effect, the distinction that Freire makes between the "banking concept" and the "problem-posing" types of education is a useful way of delimiting the conditions under which education is liberal in spirit.

LIBERAL VALUES IN HIGHER EDUCATION

When liberal education is missing, the acquisition of knowledge becomes intellectualism severed from cultivation of the whole person and from the virtues of compassion and civic virtue. Americans love to hate the forms of intellectualism that are expressed as the disembodied scholarship of ivory tower academics. But, our society is now permeated by a cold environment of technique, procedure, money, and management, all of it based on the belief that mechanism alone, severed from the beating heart of real life, can explicate the perennial concern that humans have had to find meaning in life.

Liberal education is supposed to equip citizens with humanistic values, but when schools fail to provide the necessary environment for liberal education to unfold, we can readily observe the products of that failure. We see it in forms of education that have devolved into either equipping elites with the veneer of "culture," or into training workers to serve as functionaries in a modern bureaucracy—corporate, governmental, military, or ecclesiastical. Neither the accumulation of the accoutrements of culture, nor the technical training required to become "productive" in a modern economy can be classified as "education." The original Latin *educare*—leading out or drawing forth—referred to a process of transformation. True education, in the liberal tradition, involves "drawing forth" the genuine self from the morass of ego. Without that crucial core that is shared with democracy, education becomes mere content. It lacks engagement with any part of us other than mind. It lacks the depth dimension that leads us beyond mere knowledge to *phronesis*—practical wisdom.

A simple romantic protest against a narrowly technical orientation in Western culture is also a far cry from liberal education. Where modern education is viewed as excessively "objective," some reformers have merely flown to the opposite pole, adopting pure "subjectivity" as a counterpoint. Much of "alternative education," permissive child rearing, and modern attempts at "free expression" in art have shared this quality of an entirely negative counterpoint to the rigidity of mainstream education, without any positive conception or ideal. Liberal education, by contrast, is based on a set of constructive norms of how life should be lived and how society should be organized to achieve that end.

Nevertheless, one of the great strengths of democracy in the United States is its long tradition of liberal education, a resource that is often overlooked. The rich and pluralistic system of higher education in the U.S. was centered historically on the commitment of colleges and universities to liberal education. Even the land grant colleges, created under the Morrill Act in the 19th century to democratize education and make it practical, aimed at developing a community of critical inquiry that was liberal in spirit. As Justin Morrill said in a speech after a quarter century of experience with these new state colleges:

> It was a liberal education that was proposed. Classical studies were not to be excluded, and, therefore, must be included. The Act of 1862 proposed a system of broad education by colleges, not limited to a superficial and dwarfed training, such as might be supplied by a foreman of a workshop or by a foreman of an experimental farm... The fundamental idea was to offer an opportunity in every State for a liberal and larger education to larger numbers.[7]

Even within the context of a program aimed explicitly at finding solutions to practical problems, which included vocational, technical, and paraprofessional programs, the American commitment to liberal education is evident to varying degrees across the broad spectrum of institutions that award the baccalaureate degree. Certainly liberal education is tepid in many programs, at best a kind of lip service paid to the requirement that students take "distribution" or "general education" courses on their way to specialization in the major. In many public and private colleges and universities liberal education is spoken of as becoming "well-rounded," or developed as a "whole person" and someone who has become a "lifelong learner." Other places more ambitiously engage students in active learning, experiential learning, and service learning, all variously mixed in the name of liberal education. What is noteworthy is the fact that almost every college and university still feels compelled to pay homage to the ideal of liberal arts. The American system of higher education is highly diverse, but it is held together by the commitment to liberal education and the democratic spirit that underlies it.

Considering the great diversity of approaches to liberal education in American higher education, two factors immediately stand out. First, what works in one place does not necessarily work in another. A survey of institutions that aspire to practice liberal education would show that it is practiced more or less successfully in different settings—demographically, institutionally, pedagogically. From that observation, a conclusion emerges that some might find disconcerting: there is no one formula, no universal technique, no single scale by which to measure its intensity. That is why, as Whitehead pointed out long ago, the current enthusiasm for assessment through quantitative measures and standardized teaching is dangerous:

> The proper function of a university is the imaginative acquisition of knowledge....A university is imaginative or it is nothing—at least nothing useful. Imagination is a contagious disease. It cannot be measured by the yard, or weighed by the pound, and then delivered to the students by members of the faculty. It can only be communicated by a faculty whose members themselves wear their learning with imagination.... It must not be supposed that the output of a university in the form of original ideas is solely to be measured by printed papers and books labeled with the names of their authors.... For some of the most fertile minds composition in writing, or in a form reducible to writing, seems to be an

impossibility.... Some of the more brilliant teachers are not among those who publish. Their originality requires for its expression direct intercourse with their pupils in the form of lectures or personal discussion.[8]

When the fruits of imagination are wrested from the context in which they originated, it is yet another universalization that violates the local circumstances in which alone life can be lived with richness and grace. It is scientism that is in the process of eclipsing the humanities side of Western culture. In this respect, liberal education is like love, justice, beauty, goodness, truth, and those other essential qualities of life—including democracy—that insist on remaining ineffable. These are very real but not susceptible to any final or universal statement, always working together with the "local knowledge" of particular situations. It is an art and not a science.

The second factor worth considering about the presence of liberal education in American colleges and universities is that a student or a professor could *miss* a liberal education even in those institutions where it is most vigorously practiced. Liberal education can never be done *to* one. Just because a college or university has a great curriculum or an excellent faculty, this does not guarantee that liberal education is occurring. It requires choice and conscious engagement by both students and professors; it must be identified as something valuable, and a commitment must be made. A liberal education must be *claimed*.[9]

COMPLEMENTARITY VS. DUALISM

Everything I have said so far is based on a set of premises I have yet to reveal. Once I make those premises explicit, it will be possible to gain a deeper understanding of the meaning and value of liberal education. Since I also began by claiming that liberal education is constitutive of democracy, this deeper understanding will also disclose new dimensions of that political practice. What follows, then, is a reconsideration of liberal education from the standpoint of our post-traditional moment.

Universality of cultural disciplines

For most of the last 2,500 years, from the Axial Period of the 5th century BCE until very recently, which I shall call the "traditional period of human history," there was an element of social existence that was taken for granted within every major civilization. There was universal recognition that human maturity does not unfold as a natural process, unlike what happens in most other species of animals. Every culture presupposed that bringing human beings to the fullness of their development required cultivation—a consciously employed discipline of transformation. Liberal education was the Western form of that process.

Throughout history and across cultures, disciplines of cultivation have taken many forms. Some have focused on physical disciplines with a spiritual dimension, such as athletics or yoga. Others have been dedicated to ritual performance, such as the Confucian tradition of honoring ancestors in East Asia. Jews, Christians, and Muslims have offered intellectual and spiritual mastery of a religious tradition as a way of gaining maturity. The study of revered writings—the classics of various traditions—has often served as a vehicle for making the personal journey into adulthood. All of them have been spiritual in the sense that they envision a transformation of ordinary human capacities.

Beneath the variety of these disciplines of cultivation, there has always been attention to *practice*, as the kind of activity that gives rise to nothing less than the fullness of ourselves. And along with this attention there has been distinction between this fundamentally human kind of activity and the other activities in which we engage for *productive* reasons, in order to make or cause or control. As distinct from the productive activities, the cultivation of humans has been articulated in the West as "an end in itself," or as something that is "good for its own sake."

These potentially confusing phrases point to a central truth in human life as it was envisioned during the "traditional period": that cultivation of the mature form of human being requires renunciation of all extrinsic or instrumental purpose. Coming to the fullness of who we really are is good in a way that is quite independent of whatever pleasure or pain might follow as a consequence, whatever advantage or disadvantage, whatever gain or loss as measured by the society in which one lives.

Liberal education: cultural discipline holding two poles in tension

The tradition of liberal education that arose in Europe is one example of a transformative cultural discipline that involves particular practices. Specifically, the practice of liberal education requires holding in tension two strands of Western tradition: ideas and relationships, or inherited ideals or principles and responsiveness to new conditions. Holding these two together has been a challenge, and it is possible to distinguish many of the typical problems of Western education and culture by what happens when they become separated. The history of education during the past century has exemplified this tension between "traditional" and "progressive" modes of pedagogy. The latter has sometimes been called "experiential" or "alternative" and has often been defined negatively, in opposition to the formalism of liberal education. On the one hand, the tradition in liberal education of gaining a sense of self by studying the classics in Greek and Latin was criticized as being only the delivery of ideas to be memorized and banked away for future use. In other words, it ran the danger of being all about "ideas," without any "relationship" to present realities. On the other hand, the progressive approach has had a tendency toward becoming incoherent and/or relativistic, either reflecting the whims of contemporary culture and politics or adopting an unexamined ideology of opposition. Progressive education and politics thus ran the risk of being all "relationship," based on immediate experience, with no guiding "ideas." This conflict manifests a fundamental dichotomy in Western culture between theory and practice, mind and body, conservatives and liberals, Plato and Aristotle, and even Athens and Jerusalem.

When social leaders in the liberal tradition have achieved maturity, they have been able to hold ideas and relationships in tension, without allowing one to overshadow the other. They have then been able to fulfill the vision of complementarity or synergy that creates a strong and creative culture. During much of Western history, however, the creative tension was lost, and society fell back into immature understanding based on oppositional thinking and binaries of tradition versus experimentation or tyranny versus anarchy.

An unbalanced reverence for ideas as abstract concepts has led to intellectualism, mentalism, Cartesianism, or logocentrism. These are the tendencies that have been strenuously criticized by post-Enlightenment thinkers in the late 20th century as the root of many problems in the history of the West. However, an appreciation for ideas can have the opposite effect if ideas are experienced as the outgrowth of relationships and direct experiences. Ideas in that full sense represent unmediated existential insights, and the articulation of them in such a way brings us to the critical state out of which transformation occurs. That distinctive state has been described as *aporia* or *wonder,* a state in which we can actually tune ourselves to greater harmony with reality. *Aporia* is a state of not-knowing, a state of being beyond abstract knowing, in which one achieves a condition of "knowing that I know nothing" in the Socratic sense. This is not, however, a state of ignorance or skepticism, but rather a state in which one experiences something like the *source* of knowing as distinct from merely things that are known. It is a state of wonder — as in Socrates' "philosophy begins in wonder." [10] This is not detached knowledge in which knower and known are experienced as separate entities. Instead, it is primary knowledge gained from participation, of being in the water as opposed to watching someone swim. It is a state of being energized through direct contact with a source, with a quality of life that is better captured by verbs than nouns, with an indescribable but essential *energy* that is paradoxically both the energy of the universe and the energy of one's genuine self. Ideas, in this full and nonderivative sense, can be thought of on the analogy of valves, as openings through which life-energy flows, so that the joy of real thinking can be understood by its proximity to creativity itself. There is little resemblance between this experience and the entertainment of inert concepts.

Needleman, Cushman, and Hadot[11] have all described an ancient understanding of philosophy as a guide to life that comports with the notion of nonderivative ideas as the basis of *aporia*. They remind us of an understanding of Socrates and Western philosophy that was largely eclipsed by doctrinal readings of Plato for most of the period since the death of Socrates. We can particularly thank Needleman for reinvigorating the wisdom of the Western tradition by presenting the power of Socratic knowledge before the anti-relational and intellectualist tendencies of Plato took root.

Relationship, the other pole of the liberal tradition, also has a tendency to drift toward an unbalanced state that consists of relativism, indeterminacy, and assimilation. Liberal education and democracy seek to keep it in balance with ideas. When relationship is developed in its own full sense, in collaboration with ideas, it enables one to be active as one's real self and for ideas to come alive and be radiant. The kind of relationship that permits this condition to be realized is beyond transaction or exchange, manipulation, command, power and interest, negotiation, and contract. It transcends all of the usual senses of relationship that, in the West, drive toward either sad isolation or dangerous fusion, either individualism or collectivism. As with ideas, the doorway to understanding the kind of relationship that is essential to liberal education (and democracy) is *paradox*. Within a relationship in which commonality and distinctiveness are maximized simultaneously, we experience being present in our genuineness. In mutuality, we experience thriving and the locus of our fulfillment as human beings. Yet, without the discipline and definiteness of ideas, as well as their inspirational quality, relationality loses discipline and direction. The possibility of genuine relationship is drowned by the insincere pleasantness of our era. Social exchange becomes susceptible to the relativism expressed by the insouciance of teenage indifference, contained in the favorite word of a generation: "Whatever."

In the vision of liberal education and democratic society, ideas apart from relationships become dogmas — hard and closed objects, basically weapons and/or containers. Similarly, relationships without ideas drift toward either sentimentality or manipulative opportunism, unanchored by well-examined commitment and purpose. We might also think of the tension between ideas and relationships in the following way: relationships permit us to participate in groups and to fit in by conforming to social norms, whereas ideas set us apart by causing us to question those norms with respect to more general values we might hold. To side with relationship alone is tantamount to joining an unthinking mob (people who take actions together they would fear to do alone). To side with ideas alone is to withdraw from the world into pure abstract theory, imagining how the world might have been otherwise, but not participating in it.

The balance found in Socrates

The classical statement of proper unification of ideas and relationship, and the practice through which they each come to fullness, is presented by Socrates in the *Apology*. The center of it is his famous statement that the unexamined life is not worth living. Actually, his statement is much fuller than this, and can be seen as the core practice of both liberal education and democratic culture:

> I tell you that to let no day pass without discussing goodness and the other subjects about which you hear me talking and examining both myself and others is really the very best thing that a person can do and that life without this sort of examination is not worth living.[12]

What does Socrates mean? First of all, he claims that "this sort of examination" is "the very best thing" that a person can do. For Socrates, this examination is the central discipline of human transformation. Everything else of value in human life follows from this root practice. Second, the currency of examination is "goodness and the other subjects." Here, he is talking about ideas that really matter to us, since the violation of those ideas in our daily conduct would mean that we are untrue to ourselves. The idea of "goodness" for Socrates was not an abstract topic or disinterested academic subject, but rather a matter of immediate and practical concern.

In the same dialogue, Socrates distinguishes "goodness" from both "wealth" and "fame" as goals around which people tend to organize their lives. Ideas, in the Socratic understanding, are much closer to *values*, or organizing principles of life that compel action, than they are to mere concepts that one might accept or reject dispassionately. In contemporary America, ideas are thought to be inner psychological states that are privately held. They make us unique and lead to isolation — to "the infinite regress of motive,"[13] as Hannah Arendt put it. By contrast, Socrates presupposed that ideas converge and bring us to that which is common, because they are derived from a life of shared experiences. Indeed, the overwhelming difference between the method of analysis employed by Socrates and contemporary forms of therapy, which are oriented to exploration of inner psychological states, becomes most clear when we compare results, specifically the intensity of life-energy that becomes available through the process. Many forms of therapy are only extensions of individualism that further strengthen self-control. Their capacity for true liberation is often low because private therapy offers no means to deal with ideas as social values rather than private feelings.

We can imagine that Socrates would have been puzzled by modern, private therapy. It stifles the power of ideas that need to be released by reinforcing the illusion that ideas or values are "inside" us. Liberation demands the specific kind of relationship invoked by Socrates. In the quotation from the *Apology*, he refers to "examining both myself and others." On the one hand, he does not advocate introspection or isolated reflection, which is often derisively called "navel gazing." On the other hand, Socrates does not propose that we simply accept pronouncements from authority figures. His approach to self-understanding is mutual. Relational knowledge is gained by saying what we each really think about the ideas or values we pursue together—goodness, justice, love, and subsets of these—but only if they are of real concern in our lives, and not merely academic subjects or intellectual puzzles. Mutuality allows us to arrive at the crucial moment of *aporia* or wonder, when we help one another discover that we do not, in fact, know what we thought we knew. That is the moment when the synergy between idea and relationship, between abstract knowledge and experience, begins to release an energy within the self that is the source of real growth. It is the energy Socrates speaks of as access to the "divine sign," *daimon,* or "inner voice,"[14] which we can interpret as the fundamental genuineness, integrity, or authenticity of the person. Practice of the examined life is "the very best thing a person can do" because it gives birth to the fully developed person. This is why Socrates was known as a midwife.

We can be certain that Socrates did not intend the social process of self-examination to be a private investigation of personal motives because he presupposed at all times that important action takes place in the *agora,* the public sphere. Thus, the "examined life" was always about participation in discussions about how to live together, not how to manage one's household. In this respect, we can see how advocates of liberal education understood the Socratic way as an initiation into the conversation out of which democratic culture is woven. The analysis of Michael Oakeshott provides an excellent example of how the conversation that takes place as part of liberal education forms the bedrock of democratic communication:

> Perhaps we may think [of the components of a culture] as voices, each the expression of a distinct and conditional understanding of the world and a distinct idiom of human self-understanding, and of the culture itself as these voices joined, as such voices could only be joined,

> in a conversation—an endless unrehearsed intellectual adventure in which, in imagination, we enter into a variety of modes of understanding the world and ourselves and are not disconcerted by the differences or dismayed by the inconclusiveness of it all. And perhaps we may recognize liberal learning as, above all else, an education in imagination, an initiation into the art of this conversation in which we learn to recognize the voices.[15]

This is an entirely hopeful view of the ways in which "the art of conversation" can enable participants to recognize the value of diverse perspectives and thus contribute to the deepening of democratic processes.

But not all such conversations or dialogues are conducive to the development of the democratic spirit, as I learned a few years ago, to my chagrin. In the 1990s, I participated in an ongoing conversation at my university on the subject of multiculturalism, with the aim of making the university more open to diverse voices—in short, to make it more democratic. Within a few weeks, I became aware that some of the participants viewed this discussion as a means of staking out territory and imposing a particular vision of society on others. The individuals who adopted that stance were social scientists, and they exhibited no shame in openly revealing their assumption of cultural superiority and their unwillingness to take seriously any perspective that challenged their worldview or the methodology of their discipline. Although economists are famous for this sort of disciplinary imperialism, the parties engaged in it on this occasion encompassed other social sciences as well. The professors representing these fields were in unison on the appropriateness of imposing assumptions about the individualistic nature of personhood and the private character of "choice," as if all cultural values could be reduced to personal preferences. The task of multiculturalism, in their view, was to develop strategies to bring diverse cultures into alignment with the dominant Eurocentric culture in the U.S., offering a paternalistic hand to "traditional" cultures to guide them toward modern values of individualism, competition, economic productivity, and instrumentalism. Presumably, they would have allowed some cultural practices to be perpetuated as historic re-enactments, perhaps for the sake of making money from tourism. This revealed to me that the "melting pot" version of multiculturalism was still alive and well, and that a vision of democracy based on mutually transformative conversation was far beyond the grasp of many intellectuals.

Liberal education is a direct challenge to the arrogance of such social scientists who harbor an entrenched view of their own cultural superiority. The roots of liberal education stem from the Socratic principle of *aporia*, the humility of recognizing one's limited understanding of the world and the need for interaction with diverse perspectives in order to avoid narrowness of vision. As such, the Socratic tradition needs to be understood as one of the world's great traditions of human cultivation and transformation. Huston Smith, one of our best interpreters of the great religious traditions of the world, reinforces the living character of the Socratic way of life by referring to "Western Philosophy as a World Religion."[16] Liberal education, as one embodiment of that tradition, has a quasi-religious character, as does Confucian philosophy, in that all three — liberal education, Socratic philosophy, and Confucianism — are oriented toward transformation and enlightenment through disciplines of participatory reflection. Although a more dispassionate and alienating view of philosophy and science eventually came to dominate Western thought, in which the "subject" stands outside of the world and merely observes separate "objects," the older Pythagorean-Socratic view of engaged reflection still bursts forth from time to time.

Perhaps we go too far if we consider the possibility that this "minority report" in the Western tradition can lead to an experience that has remarkable similarities to the Buddhist description of "enlightenment," a condition in which striving, dualism, and instrumental thinking cease, and the mind is simply open to awareness of what is. Can this result arise from the co-presence of ideas and relationships, or through engagement of the conversational/dialogical practice that is common to liberal education and democracy? Socrates seems to have thought so, as this statement suggests: "Acquaintance with [the practice of true philosophy] must come rather through a long period of attendance on instruction in the subject itself and of close companionship, when suddenly, like a blaze kindled by a leaping spark, it is generated in the soul and at once becomes self-sustaining."[17] Is this not very close to what other traditions describe as enlightenment?

MISUSING THE LIBERAL IDEAL

As I indicated above with respect to multiculturalism, any ideal may be turned against itself by partisans who approach the implementation of the ideal with a fixed idea of the proper solution. In that case, social scientists at my university seized upon a discussion of multiculturalism to champion American exceptionalism, a complete contradiction of multiculturalism.

I want to follow up with another story from the same time and place that relates to the nature of liberal education. During the period when our university was considering the development of multicultural programs, one humanities professor wrote an article in our local review in which he denounced multiculturalism as being contrary to the tenets of liberalism. As Lockerd summarized the problem: "Required diversity education is inimical to liberal education."[18] He cited an anthology that I had compiled for a core course on "liberal studies" as the basis for his understanding of liberal education. According to Lockerd, then, my own selection of authors on liberal education offered him the basis for arguing against the position I am taking in this article. Lockerd selectively reads an excerpt from Mark van Doren, where he finds a definition of "liberal arts [as] specifically intellectual arts" of which there are only two categories: "language and mathematics." Lockerd then cites Cardinal Newman as "explicitly rejecting the suggestion that the deliberate end of liberal learning.... should be religious and moral formation."¹⁹ Based on these brief observations, Lockerd concludes that liberal education means sticking to the acquisition of basic cognitive skills and the pursuit of knowledge for its own sake. Above all that means, in his view, the rejection of multiculturalism, which he derides as "liberal doctrine" as opposed to "liberal education."

Since my aim here is not to defend multiculturalism, I will ignore that aspect of Lockerd's statement to focus on the nature of liberal education. Central to his thesis is the view that cognitive development and moral formation are in separate compartments that must be kept isolated. He is correct, in my view, that liberal education should not try to indoctrinate students in any one moral perspective. That would be a violation of liberal education. But as I discussed in the previous section on Socrates (with a brief mention of Confucius), the original aim of liberal education was to call forth a kind of enlightenment that transcends the dualism of thought and action that suffuses the Western tradition. There has been a strong tendency toward thinking of liberal education in purely intellectual terms, in which "ideas" are given priority over "relationships" at every turn, and Lockerd is a good representative of that point of view. My aim here is to suggest that liberal education as elite intellectual training in Western classics might have worked for centuries of monarchy and aristocracy, but the complementarity of ideas and relationships is essential for the sustenance of democracy. I do not regard Lockerd's view as wrong, so much as one sided.

LIBERAL EDUCATION AND DEMOCRACY IN ACTION

Thus far, we have examined the philosophical underpinnings of liberal education and what it offers to a society that values reflective dialogical processes. The health of democracy depends on the widespread capacity for collegial self-reflection about both individual aims and the collective purposes of the larger society. We turn now to the question of how to realize the goal of making liberal education broadly available. This is not simply a question of how to repackage an old product, since each generation must find a way to reappropriate the values of liberal education using its own idioms. This requires both an appreciation of past forms by which this ancient tradition was transmitted and present forms that can bring it to life anew.

If the issues I raise were simply private ruminations, they would influence only those who happen to read my thoughts in books or articles. Fortunately, there are many people and groups in the United States who are dedicated to preserving liberal education both as training for a reflective life and as one of the cornerstones of democracy. There are at least three national associations devoted to the support of liberal education, and they influence the activities of many colleges and universities that seek to uphold the ideals of this tradition. The three associations are:

- The American Association of Colleges and Universities (AAC&U: www.aacu.org)—an association, based in Washington, D.C., of "nearly 1,400 member institutions—including accredited public and private colleges, community colleges, research universities, and comprehensive universities of every type and size," all of which "are committed to extending the advantages of a liberal education to all students."

- The Society for Values in Higher Education (SVHE: www.svhe.org)—founded in 1922 to promote the teaching of religious studies in higher education; since the 1970s focused more broadly on interdisciplinary and values-conscious teaching that encourages students and faculty to grapple directly with moral issues, both in and out of the classroom. It is currently based at Western Kentucky University in Bowling Green.

- The Council on Public Liberal Arts Colleges (COPLAC: www.coplac.org)—founded in 1987, based at the University of North Carolina, Asheville; consists of 30 North American colleges and universities that collaborate in promoting the "benefits of... comprehensive public higher education in the liberal arts and sciences."

Although these associations have different missions and constituencies, they are astonishingly consistent in their understanding of the relationship between liberal education and democracy. They share, in a broad sense, the perspective that I have outlined in which democracy is constituted by a citizenry steeped in the tension between "ideas" and "relationships." The principles espoused and the activities carried out by these associations underlines the importance of preserving forms of liberal education that keep that tension intact. Following are five categories that give more definiteness to the ideals of liberal education as it is practiced and promoted by these associations:

1. *Beyond Tolerance to Pluralism:* The United States has passed through two major transitions in its history that relate to democracy. The first was the abolition of slavery, and the second was the extension of basic political rights to widening groups of people. We are now in the midst of a third transition that involves finding the means of full inclusion of all citizens who are currently alienated from public life by social and economic barriers. To breach those barriers requires collective action to change the structures of society, not merely the elimination of restrictive laws. To achieve the next generation of social and economic rights involves a move beyond toleration or neutral acceptance to the positive affirmation of difference.

The three associations that promote liberal education are very aware that this third transformation imposes new challenges on institutions of higher education that make diversity and inclusion positive goals. That entails actions that might feel disruptive at times, because those actions challenge comfortable practices. Conscientious faculty and administrators are aware that moving beyond toleration or diversity as mere friendliness or appreciation of difference raises a host of difficult questions.

In the second transition of democracy, Americans learned to acknowledge differences. But there was always a hidden danger.

Toleration of difference can easily accommodate a mindset that views cultural differences as temporary obstacles to the eventual homogenization of world culture under the universalizing terms of modernization. That was the "melting pot" ideal of American liberal thought for many generations, one that presumed that other cultures would eventually assimilate the norms of northern European Protestantism and its approach to politics, education, and religious values. According to that view, the public realm was to be the arena of common (Protestant) values, and the private arena could contain the diversity of lifestyles at the family level. The separation of public and private spheres is a hallmark of modern thought, and it ultimately fails, as repudiation of the "melting pot" ideal testifies.

The concern now is to move into a stage of pluralism, a condition of full affirmation in which otherness is preserved and enhanced at the same time self is enhanced, along with the public space in which the encounter takes place. This is not achieved easily, as the encounter creates conflicts, putting the university at the center of painful cultural transformation. Overcoming specious forms of unity that suppress diversity is a major developmental challenge.

2. *The Social Basis of Democracy in Diversity:* At times, the academic associations devoted to liberal education make explicit the connection between diversity, democracy, and the discipline of learning how to be bridge-builders. We find this sensibility in the following statement by AAC&U:

> [It] is our conviction that democracy cannot fulfill its aspirations without acknowledging diversity and that diversity finds a moral compass in democratic values and principles...Higher education, we believe, can nurture Americans' commitment and capacity to create a society in which democratic aspirations become democratic justice and diversity proves a means of forging a deeper unity.[20]

The SVHE concurs with that assessment. SVHE defines "deliberative democracy" in higher education as a program that "engages citizens, encourages participation and collective action, and leads to meaningful, sustainable change." SVHE continues that the challenge is

> to create intentionally designed and ongoing opportunities for identifying, studying, deliberating, and acting on problems with social and ethical implications, and to draw from the work of experienced community builders and practitioners in deliberative democracy.[21]

3. *Global Interdependence and Environmental Challenges:* There was a time in the recent past when it was still possible for educators to ignore threats posed by human activities that disrupt the natural environment. Now some of the biggest challenges facing democratic societies are comprised of those destructive patterns, and the academic associations discussed above are actively responding to the situation. For example, the 2010 annual meeting of SVHE was on "Making Choices: Sustainability in a World of Conflicting Values." Cultivating "sustainability" as something more than maintenance of the status quo was also an element in the COPLAC session on "Sustaining Democracy, Sustaining the Environment: The Liberal Arts Mission" at the 2007 AACU conference.

Rather than seeing "sustainability," "democracy," and "diversity" as items on a shopping list that students are to acquire like credit hours leading to a credential, the designers of a liberal education see their aim as creating conditions under which students will experience the underlying unity of those ideals and eventually be able to articulate how they reinforce each other. The three principles contribute to a single aesthetic ideal of maximum diversity within a stable system, which is made stable because it is simultaneously open to new information and inclusive of all elements within it. That is what makes it possible to have sustainability without authoritarianism and democracy without environmental degradation.

None of this can be articulated in a way that can be handed to students as a set of ideas to grasp and memorize. The unity of the principles underlying democracy and liberal education must be acquired through a process that combines abstract ideas and personal experience. The desired outcome probably cannot be stated in traditional Western intellectual terms because there are paradoxes at the heart of this kind of dialogical knowledge that must be experienced directly to be appreciated.

4. *Service Beyond Volunteerism:* Government has many times in history had the character of warlords preying on the populace. Liberal education seeks to create a citizenry with a different vision of government: one in which government consists of people who are dedicated to serving the common good. Since all citizens are part of the governing process in a true democracy, everyone is called upon to both lead and to serve. Leadership and service lie at the root of the democratic ideal. The associations dedicated to liberal education encourage this by promoting "service learning," experiences in which students learn by engaging in activities that serve the community. As Dawn Michele Whitehead notes:

> By providing an anchor for active involvement with diverse communities engaged in real-world challenges, global service-learning experiences can support the achievement of such learning outcomes as civic knowledge and intercultural knowledge and competence—outcomes that the Association of American Colleges and Universities (AAC&U) has deemed "essential" in the twenty-first century.[22]

The hope is that participating students and faculty in these programs will develop "civic virtue," or active care for the commonly shared life and the open space of encounter, which not only provides a service to others but is also a discipline or practice by which individuals cultivate their own humanity. In terms of the great religious traditions, this is the point at which "return" takes place, in which the wise elder teaches the next generation needed skills rather than drifting off in to private mystical states. The challenge for those who have gained the benefits of liberal education is to find some way to serve the community with their wisdom. As Martin Luther King, Jr. put it:

> An individual has not started living fully until they can rise above the narrow confines of individualistic concerns to the broader concerns of humanity. Every person must decide at some point, whether they will walk in light of creative altruism or in the darkness of destructive selfishness. This is the judgment: "Life's most persistent and urgent question is, what are you doing for others?"[23]

The need to transcend selfishness is not simply a matter of individual morality. In the context of liberal education, "civic engagement" and "service" transcend their usual connotations because they are elements in a process of self-transformation. The opening of the individual to "diversity," "sustainability," and "democracy" through service is a process that cannot be comprehended by the generic term "volunteering." The emphasis in this fourth theme is not on the *definition* of these terms, but rather on their *enactment*. That is why the lessons to be learned cannot be taught in the abstract. What matters in civic engagement is the doing of it, the practice. The relationship between theory and practice is much more complex and dynamic than it was in some older forms of liberal education that insisted that one must gain a full intellectual understanding prior to taking action. When students learn by participating in service, achieving intellectual resolution in theory is no longer a prerequisite for application in practice. Necessary principles of guidance and purpose can come from shared commitments and dense relationship, rather than from a prior static intellectual formulation.

5. *Development as Cultivation of Civic Virtue:* If the dialogical process of liberal education succeeds, the end result is a person who is engaged in the lifelong process of striving to cultivate virtue. Clearly, this involves practices and disciplines that inculcate habits extending beyond the scope of private morality, and it cannot be attained simply by the acquisition of knowledge in a classroom setting. "Critical

thinking," "reflexivity," "learning how to learn," and "dialogue" are all important components of the process of cultivating virtue, but they are just the beginning. At a level deeper than individual qualities to be developed, the active and experiential aspects of liberal education are essential in creating a life that is responsive to pluralism, sustainability, and democracy as envisioned in the previous themes. This, in turn, involves growing into the more complex and dynamic orientation to the intellect, and greater attentiveness to the wisdom that arises out of practice and relationship.

How can colleges and universities teach students the necessary skills to become lifelong cultivators of civic virtue? This may be one of the most difficult tasks for a school to undertake, since there is no specific locus for this type of development in the standard curriculum. How exactly do students overcome and unlearn the simple truths of popular culture and develop an appreciation of the ambiguity of all knowledge? The premise of liberal education is that every student has the capacity for this sort of moral development based on Socratic wisdom and engagement. But each student must confront the choice about how to respond to the challenge.

The influential work of Perry[24] describes a developmental movement that occurs in the passage through college by way of a tacit curriculum that emerges from dialogue in the classroom that challenges the preconceptions that students bring with them. This "tacit curriculum" is not described in catalogues or course descriptions, and yet it is the primary form of learning that takes place. If the development process is successful, the student progresses through three stages: 1) absolutism, 2) relativism, and 3) commitment.

In the first, or absolutist, stage, students enter a university from high school or a community college with the belief that there is a right answer for every intellectual problem and that textbooks have authority. Some students realize that there are problems for which no answer is accepted by all experts, in which case the student may be challenged to find out which expert has the right answer. The central feature of the stage of absolutism is the certainty that right answers exist somewhere, even if they are not yet available. Regarding every mystery, the absolutist might say: "Science does not know yet, but eventually science will explain it."

In the second stage, in which a relativist orientation develops, the recognition that there are problems without known solutions leads a student to understand that knowledge is contested and that truth-claims are a result of one's perspective. There are multiple sources of authority that ask questions in different ways. Students at this stage let go of the need to have certainty and take a step into unfamiliar territory in which "correct" answers may not exist. Venturing beyond the fixed truths of absolutism creates a crisis. Some students will reject the ambiguity they now face and retreat to a world of certainty, but never with the same naïve confidence as before. Others will adopt a relativistic view that all truth is subjective, that every form of truth is equally valid, and that the triumph of one idea over another is based purely on power dynamics. Another strategy in response to ambiguity is to compartmentalize knowledge so that conflicting ideas stay separated from each other. A scientist who performs painful experiments on animals during the day and comes home to care for a favorite pet at night would be an example of this compartmentalization. This strategy is probably the dominant one in modern culture. Thus, many students who take part in liberal education travel from the wholeness of absolutism to the fragmentation of relativism without advancing to a new stage of synthesis.

In the third stage, the student develops a commitment to a particular perspective, at least provisionally. An absolutist makes a pseudo-commitment, which involves a reversion to the first level and a decision to avoid ambiguity, side with authority, and dismiss other perspectives. That is not really a commitment because it entails giving up personal autonomy and allowing others to decide on one's behalf. True commitment derives from pluralism — respect for the multiplicity of perspectives in the world and the partial validity of each of them. This involves an affirmation that a person makes consciously, knowing the limits of his or her own knowledge. Commitments, according to Perry, are acts of choice that "require the courage of responsibility, and presuppose an acceptance of human limits, including the limits of reason."[24]

A society in which there is a reservoir of civic virtue among citizens is a prerequisite for true democracy to flourish. That reservoir is replenished only if enough members of society go through a process of moral development outlined above, in which they reach the stage of commitment and understand the moral demands of living in a pluralistic society. We can now see precisely why liberal education is a core element of democracy. Without it, the members of society may have technical competence and a capacity for understanding complex policy issues, but few would develop the practices and disciplines that make possible civic virtue.

It is precisely the attainment of the third stage of moral development arising from liberal education that makes it possible for us to grow beyond intellectualism and the world of ideology, to enter a relational/democratic world. Citizens are then able to make reasoned commitments, while at the same time maintaining awareness of their limitations and the possibility of further refinement and growth. The ability to tolerate ambiguity, which emerges in the third stage, enables citizens to thrive in relationships of simultaneous similarity and difference, without resorting to the antinomy of reductive sameness or complete incommensurability.

The five themes we have just considered form the basis of most contemporary discussions of how to put liberal education into practice and the ways in which liberal education serves to strengthen democracy. Thus, the associations that are working to preserve and develop liberal education are working to maintain an open, democratic society as surely as organizations that work to protect constitutional rights. Indeed, without social support for civic culture, the meaning of the Constitution would be lost after a few generations. For that reason, continuing support for liberal education is imperative, particularly in response to efforts to conform all of higher education to a business model of measurable objectives.

THE PROCESS OBSERVED

Thus far, I have spoken about the nature of liberal education from afar, from the perspective of a distant observer. But that is not how I know about it. I have been privileged to experience the joy of learning and transformation that accompanies liberal education from the perspective of a participant. At this point, I want to relate how I have encountered the democratic potential of liberal education specifically in the context of a course on philosophy. A major part of my task in that situation is to be present as a guide but to overcome the expectations that students have of professors as authority figures.

In the course, we begin with a question derived from experience that forces us to think and to notice our feelings about the importance of truth or what gives life value. The first step in any inquiry is to pay attention to one's own thinking, simply by asking oneself and listening for sincere response. Often we do not even know what we are looking for. This step includes toleration of the *aporia*, the experience described earlier of realizing that I "know nothing." Whatever our response, it is likely to be tentative and humble. Once we have some sense of where we stand, it then becomes possible to turn to sources, to others who present their answers to the same questions, like Socrates, or Lao Tzu, or Aristotle, as well as one's classmates, professor(s), and contemporary sources. Through comparison and contrast, agreement and disagreement, the presence of others helps us refine our thinking. The process often creates a mysterious opening of horizons, which is when real thinking begins.

Undoubtedly, some educators who are more comfortable in a traditional role as the purveyor of knowledge will criticize the relational or dialogical approach that I am describing. Yet, students ultimately learn more in an environment in which they listen to others and read original sources to find answers to real questions, especially when compared to rote learning. Through the back and forth approach to learning, both students and teachers become clearer and more articulate about our own stance on important questions, even as we become more comfortable with the condition of *aporia* and use it as an opening through which wisdom enters our lives. We also gain flexibility in our positions as we also learn to appreciate and respect the positions of others. Here is the practice through which learning moves beyond *in*-formation to *trans*-formation. As we learn by and from each other, we are transformed through the spirit in which the encounter occurs.

From repeated engagement in a process that involves questioning of oneself and others, we emerge as different persons. We are transformed. We know ourselves in a new way that is not self-centered; we are fully involved in the world but not co-opted by it; we continue to seek our own private ends, but we are now more cooperative and respectful of the relationships in which transformation becomes possible. In all of these ways, we learn to balance our own aims with the common good. As we become familiar and comfortable with this process, we become independent, lifelong learners both in school and outside. A few who go through this process become truly magnificent, enlightened human beings. Even the faculty who go through this process with students again and again attain a higher degree of self-understanding with each experience. There is no end to the journey.

When we start the process at the beginning of a course, it is not easy. Many students are anxious and skeptical, even if they have had some previous experience. They doubt they can learn anything in this non-traditional way. So, there is a lot of resistance, which is itself instructive. The predisposition of most contemporary American students is toward either the objective or the subjective pole. On the objective side, they want to know what information they are supposed to learn and what will be "on the test?" When they encounter questions for which there are no "right" answers, students tend to go to the opposite pole of subjectivity. At that stage, they imagine the professors are asking them to express their feelings or else to respond to the equally subjective likes and dislikes of the professor. Those are the poles of experience they have learned to recognize.

To provide the framework for a new kind of learning, something like "patterned learning" is required. Just as a physical trainer might move an athlete's body into the correct position, we do something analogous in the learning of inquiry. We find various ways to pattern the behavior as a process, not in terms of content. Student then learn to exercise these unfamiliar "muscles" without at first understanding why. (The scene in the movie *The Karate Kid,* where Mr. Miyagi teaches Daniel's mind-body a defensive maneuver by having him sand the deck is an example of this.) Often they do not trust this applied learning process until they write papers and see for themselves what they have learned and who they have become.

At that moment of awareness, students can see that they have learned to integrate knowledge from others with their personal experiences. They begin to see from experience that it is possible to break through the objective-subjective dichotomy and arrive at a new paradigm of understanding. Their thought becomes less simplistic and oppositional as they move toward synergistic explorations. They discover a relational world in which there are no objectively right answers and no arguments with just two sides, but they also learn that subjective feelings do not provide adequate guidance either. If the practice is well-rooted, it will, like any genuinely transformative practice, expand from the more narrow and protected environment of the classroom to a way of being and relating in all of life, developing a truly democratic way of living. The more narrow disciplines of reading/listening, writing/speaking, and inquiry/conversation/dialogue break open into a way of being in the world.

A DEMOCRATIC CURRICULUM

How does an account of the inner workings of liberal education provide insights into how we might learn to reappropriate the democratic spirit in America?

We tend to think of liberal education as a process that takes place in colleges and universities, and it is indeed most concentrated there. That is the normal location where individuals encounter it and are trained in it. But perhaps it could also be applied to American culture as a whole in the pursuit of democratic practices and civic morality. Not everyone will have a chance to purchase an expensive liberal arts degree. For those outside of university life, it would serve a powerful purpose to discover a medium for engagement and deliberation on the challenges of American public life. Those challenges include not only political issues regarding the permeable boundary between public and private realms but also questions about how to organize our personal lives in relation to growing global concerns about sustainability and equity.

Liberal education can be seen as a sort of metacurriculum of American culture, with classrooms among the most effective and healthy public spaces we have in America. This is the case in both the idea and the relationship aspects of liberal education discussed earlier in this chapter. The primary ideas are those of democracy, diversity, development, and sustainability; and relationships center on the aim of including the widest possible diversity of fellow-learners, not only within educational institutions but also in the broader local and global communities.

We have seen liberal education addressing two issues in particular, both of which are arguably the deepest and most basic issues of America culture in our time.

The first issue is that of inclusion and diversity. The question we face at present is whether liberal education can enable us to grapple with the third great crisis of American history, the affirmation of economic and social rights commensurate with the political rights that have been won. Liberal education, by its nature, fosters a discussion based on the ideal of unity in diversity, but, as a practical matter, that ideal has not yet been fully articulated and embraced. Nevertheless, it remains a subtext in various situations. The fact that this ideal stimulates conflict in the larger culture is an important reason to make it a central part of liberal education. A good example is Erin O'Connor's account of the controversy about the assignment of Barbara Ehrenreich's *Nickel and Dimed: On (Not) Getting By in America* in freshman orientation programs at a number of colleges and universities. O'Connor says that "on both sides of the debate [about the appropriateness of this reading], a book's politics are assumed to matter more than its scholarly merit or literary quality." She concludes by sharing the fear that "in the name of eliminating 'bias,' American education has been reduced to a banal exercise in multicultural appeasement."[26] Nothing could be further from the heart of liberal education than conformity and banality, particularly when addressing an issue that is central to democracy.

The second issue that liberal education faces is how to conceive of culture in balanced terms rather than as a single-minded pursuit of the intellect and its achievements. This issue encompasses questions about the balance between the natural sciences and the humanities in higher education, the proper role of humans vis-à-vis nature in agriculture and industry, and competing values involved in new technologies. It also casts doubt on fixed and rigid ideological positions that define the person. Discussions about the practice of liberal education entail a developmental movement from a traditional intellectual culture to a relational worldview. Nostalgic reverence for strict adherence to the received Western canon of knowledge has become loaded with conservative ideology, but progressive thought has qualities that are simply an inversion of that conservatism. In educational terms, the 20th century was saddled with an antinomy of "traditional education," which simply delivered intellectual products, versus "alternative education" that gave too much weight toward personal feelings and self-expression. Dewey attempted to correct that dualism by critiquing both poles of the conflict and proposing a more integrated approach, similar to the one I described earlier in terms of Socratic transcendence of idea and relationship.

Mutual engagement with ideas and methods, and critical reflection as a group on relevant issues is the heart of the relational paradigm. The intellect has a role to play, but not always as a leader. It can point to adjustments of action and practice that contribute to the maximizing of democracy, diversity, development, and sustainability. But, in doing so, the intellect is never the framework within which mutuality and communication occur. It plays only a supportive role by expanding the conditions under which mutual learning is possible. It can contribute by making critical judgments by invoking historical precedent or methods of evaluation. Rather than standing aloof and managing events from afar, the intellect becomes fully engaged in activity along with imagination, skills of moral development, and experiential insights. Ideas are not relegated to a second-class status. Instead, they are no longer allowed to operate in ungrounded ways as pure theory. Bringing ideas back into the world of experience, we enable ideas to regain their transformative power in democratic life, a process that rarely happens in the rarified air of the *laissez-faire* exchange of ideas in the context of Western individualism.

DISPLACING LIBERAL EDUCATION

There is nothing inevitable about cultural support for liberal education. Like democracy, it is a fragile flower that blooms only under limited conditions. Moreover, those conditions do not obtain by accident. They have to be sustained by conscious effort and design. We have been fortunate in the United States to have been founded by leaders who valued liberal education and by generations of leaders who sought to expand the experience of liberal education as broadly as possible. That is the reason the American experiment in democracy has lasted as long as it has. Liberal education will always stand in opposition to a culture that prizes nothing more than commercial success. There is nothing antithetical to liberal education in commerce itself, and top business leaders have for much of American history recognized that their success depended in part on a culture that valued imagination and innovation, habits of mind more likely to emerge from liberal education than from training in narrowly defined business skills. But a growing body of opinion in the United States today rejects the liberal vision and insists that universities should be more practical and business-like. This view has already affected the legislatures of many states. For the critics of liberal education in America today, talk of ideas, relationships, and transformation are just rhetorical devices that naïve professors use to extract money from the public, without having to provide any useful service in return.

The desire to make higher education practical and to serve the interests of the economy is not a new idea. The creation of land grant colleges and universities in the 19th century was motivated in part by that desire. However, there was also a self-conscious aim to ensure that those land grant institutions offered a balance of courses and inculcated the spirit of liberal education to the extent possible. Many a 19th century farmer was brought up on the works of Shakespeare and Melville, as well as on principles of crop fertilization. They would have objected to a university that offered nothing more than training programs in technical skills.

Other waves of practical reform of higher education have crossed America, either to avoid a one-sided intellectualism that too easily becomes lost in abstraction or to insist that education should be evaluated by whether students are learning anything "useful," a term often left undefined. In our own day, the primary way of framing the issue is in terms of financial criteria: is it a good return on investment? In the wake of the Great Recession of 2008, that question has been raised by numerous authors, including Hacker and Dreifus, "born-again Jeffersonians" who believe that "higher education should be open to every young person."[27] At least when they ask if higher education is worth the investment, they oppose transforming universities into vocational schools, and they balk at schools that are top-heavy with administrators and the vast number of non-educational programs that universities now offer. To them the "return" on educational investment is overall development as a person, very much in the tradition of liberal education.

Although the reforms suggested by Hacker and Dreifus would provide the basic elements of liberal education for every student who wanted them, the majority of authors engaged in the debate about college as an investment have much more pecuniary ideas about how to measure the success of higher education. They ask, "Does it pay for itself in higher future salaries, and is it worth going to college at all?" Some, like William Gross, managing director of Pacific Investment Management Company, argue that American students are wasting their minds by going to college, and that "All of us who have been there [Duke in his case] know an undergraduate education is primarily a four-year vacation interrupted by periodic bouts of cramming or Google plagiarizing."[28] David Leonhardt counters with a statistical demonstration that people with a college degree make substantially more money, even in jobs that do not require the degree,[29] but his argument presupposes that Gross and others are correct in making a financial return the right issue to raise.

In this important debate over the future of higher education, the role of liberal education in creating the conditions necessary for democracy is almost entirely ignored. Also left out are all considerations about the kind of persons a nation should strive to cultivate. In that respect, the debate has conceded the inevitability of living within the abyss of modern values and measuring the value of civilization solely in terms of per capita income. If that is where the discussion ends, then it is certain that nihilism has won, since nihilism is simply the view that there is "nothing more" to life than observable relationships and social conventions. The death of Socrates is a reminder that nihilism can gain the upper hand even in a society that seemingly values wisdom. But because there is an element of bad faith in nihilism, its advocates never rest with ease. Thus, some of the nihilists of our time are uncomfortable with the conclusion that money and power should be thought of as ultimate values.

We can hope, therefore, that even the most ardent proponent of objective evaluation of education might recognize there is some validity when Carol Schneider, President of AAC&U, took to task the National Governors Association when it issued a report that effectively equated higher education with job training. As Schneider commented: "The report might at least acknowledge that governors are elected by citizens and that higher education plays a vital role in building civic capacity."[30] No doubt the toughest argument to make to the educational bureaucrat would be in support of Deresiewicz, who argues that a college education should instill the character traits of leaders: independent judgment, moral courage, and concentrated thinking.[31] Because nihilism is a product of bad faith, it is held in place by an unwillingness to confront the sneaking suspicion that values cannot be pinned to a board like dead butterflies. In effect, the technocrats who thrive in a nihilistic environment become annoyed by reminders that butterflies can only be fully understood in life, not as dead objects. Because nihilism is suffused with this bad faith, there is a resentment and an impatience to it, and an insistence that others join them in their conclusion. It is as though they dimly recall something they once believed in and then gave up on in disappointment, a sense that they had been betrayed or duped. This kind of experience leads to intolerance of those who still believe, and possibly even a wish to dismiss them in some aggressive way.

This understanding of the enemies of liberal education is essential if those who see its value are to preserve it. The ability to protect liberal education will depend on reclaiming ideals that pertain to the appreciation of and aspiration toward subtle values in life. Above all, this will entail affirmation of and commitment to a vision of a better life that goes far beyond mere material comfort. Compassion is the one reliable guiding value of that vision. Few things in our common life are as important as sustaining an ongoing conversation, both intellectually and practically, as to how these ineffable values might be more fully embodied on this very fragile planet.

One of the deepest absurdities of the current state of affairs is that American universities seem to be turning their backs on the educational foundations of an informed citizenry at the very moment in history when other nations are striving to attain the values that America previously symbolized. Schneider has clearly articulated this irony: "Just as myopic policy advisors are urging a narrowing of American higher education, Asian countries are hastening to adapt our signature designs for liberal and general education."[32]

As I have argued throughout this article, the same characteristics that are the fabric of liberal education are constitutive of democracy. Whether the advocates of technocratic values in education undermine liberal education with benign neglect or open attack, the result will be the same. The conditions upon which democracy rests are being eroded.

CONCLUSION

In the midst of the crises of our time, it is easy to overlook or take for granted the enormous contribution of liberal education to the nourishment and maintenance of a democratic society. I conclude this chapter by sharing the words of Martha Nussbaum, a fellow citizen and colleague who reminds us in a most helpful way of the grandeur of what we are doing in America, of the close relationship between education and democracy, and of how America might be valued in the world community:

> Our country has embarked on an unparalleled experiment, inspired by these ideals of self-command and cultivated humanity. Unlike all other nations, we seek a higher education to contribute a general preparation for citizenship, not just a specialized preparation for a career. To a greater

degree than all other nations, we have tried to extend the
benefits of this education to all citizens, whatever their class,
race, sex, ethnicity, or religion. We hope to draw citizens
toward one another by complex mutual understanding
and individual self-scrutiny, building a democratic culture
that is truly deliberative and reflective, rather than simply
the collision of unexamined preferences. And we hope in
this way to justify and perpetuate our nation's claim to be
a valuable member of a world community of nations that
must increasingly learn how to understand, respect, and
communicate, if our common human problems are to be
constructively addressed.[33]

Indeed, the genius of America itself can be taken to exist in the interplay between "complex mutual understanding" and "individual self-scrutiny," one that must be taught and modeled in both political life and education. For the complex mutuality of democracy is impossible without the mature or transformed person. And at the same time, self-scrutiny goes astray without democratic values of social transformation, the dignity of all people, and conversation among the people as the best place to find wisdom. Democracy and liberal education need each other, for both completion and continuous correction. Indeed, as we have seen from the contemporary discussion of liberal education, they tend toward convergence, in something very much like the Confucian ideal of society as a learning community.

ENDNOTES

1. Thomas Jefferson, "Proposed Constitution of the State of Virginia," in *The Works of Thomas Jefferson in 12 Volumes: Vol. II Correspondence 1771–1779, the Summary View, and the Declaration of Independence,* edited by Paul Leicester Ford (New York: G.P. Putnam's Sons, 1776, 1904) 158–83; online: https://archive.org/details/workofjeffero2jeffuoft/.

2. Jefferson, *Notes on the State of Virginia.* (Boston: Lilly & Wait, 1782, 1832); online: https://archive.org/details/workofjeffero2jeffuoft/.

3   Alfred North Whitehead, *The Aims of Education* (New York: Free Press, 1933, 1967), 1.

4   William James, *Talks to Teachers* (New York: Henry Holt & Co., 1889); online: https://ebooks.adelaide.edu.au/j/james/william/talks/complete.html#chapter5.

5   John Dewey, *Art as Experience* (New York: Capricorn Books, 1932, 1958), 344.

6   Paulo Freire, *Pedagogy of the Oppressed* (New York: Continuum Press, 1970) 64.

7   Justin Morrill, "An address in behalf of the University of Vermont and State Agricultural College," excerpted in *The Land-Grant Tradition* (Washington, DC: National Association of State Universities and Land Grant Colleges, 1888, 1995).

8   Alfred North Whitehead, "The Aims of Education," in *The Aims of Education and Other Essays* (New York: Free Press, 1933, v967), 96, 97, 98–99.

9   See my *Claiming a Liberal Education: Resources for Realizing the College Experience* (Needham Heights, MA: Ginn, 1990).

10 Plato, *Theaetus* 155d, in *The Collected Dialogues of Plato,* ed. Edith Hamilton Cairns, Bollingen Series no. 71 (New York: Pantheon Books, 1985), 860.

11 See Jacob Needleman, *The Heart of Philosophy* (New York: Penguin, 2003); Robert Cushman, *Therapeia: Plato's Conception of Philosophy* (Westport, CT: Greenwood Press, 1958); and Pierre Hadot, *Philosophy as a Way of Life: Spiritual Exercises from Socrates to Foucault,* ed. Arnold Davidson, trans. Michael Chase (Malden, MA: Wiley-Blackwell, 1995).

12 Plato, *Apology* 38a.

13 Hannah Arendt, *The Human Condition* (Chicago: University of Chicago Press, 1958), 5.

14 Plato, *Apology* 31d, 40a.

15 Michael Oakeshott, *The Voice of Liberal Learning* (New Haven: Yale University Press, 1989), 541.

16 Huston Smith, "Western Philosophy as a World Religion." in

Transcendence and the Sacred, Alan Olson and Leroy Rouner, eds. (Notre Dame, IN: University of Notre Dame Press, 1981).

17 Plato, *Letters* VII241c-d, in *The Collected Dialogues of Plato,* 1589.

18 Benjamin G. Lockerd, Jr., "Liberal Education and Liberal Dogma." *Grand Valley Review* 7(1): 52–56; online: http://scholarworks.gvsu.edu/cgi/viewcontent.cgi?article=1596&context=gvr/.

19 Mark Van Doren, *Liberal Education* (New York: Henry Holt, 1943).

20 Jerry Gaff, *General Education: The Changing Agenda* (Washington, DC: American Association of Colleges and Universities, 1999).

21 SVHE, "The Democracy Project," Society for Values in Higher Education. Bowling Green, KY, 2011; online: http://www.svhe.org/democracyproject.html/.

22 Dawn Michele Whitehead, "Global Service Learning: Addressing the Big Challenges, *Diversity & Democracy* 18 (3); online: http://www.aacu.org/diversitydemocracy/2015/summer/whitehead/.

23 Martin Luther King, Jr., "Conquering Self-Centeredness," sermon delivered at Dexter Avenue Baptist Church, Montgomery, Alabama, August 11, in *The Papers of Martin Luther King, Jr. Volume IV: Symbol of the Movement, January 1957–December 1958,* Clayborne Carson, Susan Carson, Adrienne Clay, Virginia Shadron, and Kieran Taylor, eds. (Berkeley: University of California Press, 1957, 2000), 256.

24 William Perry, *Forms of Intellectual and Moral Development in the College Years (*New York: Holt, Rinehart and Winston, 1968), 136.

25 Perry, 135.

26 Erin O'Connor, "Misreading What Reading is For," *Chronicle of Higher Education,* 4 September 2003; https://www.chronicle.com/article/Misreading-What-Reading-Is-For/9922/.

27 Andrew Hacker and Claudia Dreifus, *Higher Education?: How Colleges are Wasting Our Money and Failing Our Kids—and What We Can Do About It* (New York: St. Martin's Press, 2010) 3.

28 William Gross, "School Daze, School Daze/Good Old Golden Rules Days," *Pimco* July 2011; https://www.pimco.com/insights/economic-and-market-commentary/investment-outlook/school-daze-school-daze-good-old-golden-rule-days/.

29 David Leonhardt, "Even for Cashiers, College Pays Off," *New York Times,* Sunday Review Section, 26 June 2011: 3.

30 Carol Geary Schneider, "'Degrees for What Jobs?' Wrong Question, Wrong Answers," *Chronicle of Higher Education,* 10 May 2011, online: http://chronicle.com/article/Degrees-for-What-Jobs-Wrong/127328/.

31 Deresiewicz, "Solitude and Leadership," *The American Scholar,* June 29, 2014, online: http://theamericanscholar.org/solitude-and-leadership/print/.

32 Schneider, "Degrees for What Jobs," 2.

33 Martha Nussbaum, *Cultivating Humanity: A Classical Defense of Reform in Liberal Education* (Cambridge: Harvard University Press, 1997), 294.

9

PRAGMATISM, POSSIBILITY, AND HUMAN DEVELOPMENT

After the final no there comes a yes
And on that yes the future world depends. –Wallace Stevens[1]

WE AMERICANS ARE "PRAGMATIC." We are practical, concerned with consequences, focused on getting things done, solving problems. So ideological gridlock does not make sense; it is the very opposite of what we like to be. Perhaps the current condition of America arises out of the fact that we also like to think of ourselves as individualists. It turns out, though, that individualism, as the belief that the common good will be the automatic result of everyone pursuing their interests, is not really working either. In fact, one of the chief ironies of our time is that individualism can itself become an ideology, a groupthink expressed as the insistence that everything be privatized. So we have frustration with ideological rigidity on the one hand, and dysfunctional individualism on the other. Together, they amount to the same attitude, eclipsing problem solving and the common good. One begins to wonder if these three — ideology, individualism, and their frequent coincidence—are symptoms of a dysfunctional worldview or some other deep cultural distress.

Our present condition is most unfortunate, since pragmatism, understood from its origin in the life experience of the absence of traditional culture, offers another possibility. It can give rise to the definite yet flexible life orientation we so desperately need in these precarious times. It can help in the broad movement of our era beyond those qualities of modernity that have rather recently been discovered to be both unsustainable and undesirable. It can facilitate development into a new global orientation that is democratic in the deep sense and inclusive of the natural world. It could even help us cope with the tragicomic qualities of the world and the improbable nature of our hope.[2] With pragmatism we can learn the crucial hermeneutical and liberationist lessons of the 20th century and survive the very rigorous transformative process through which a new worldview of peace, justice, and creativity is emerging—despite America's current paralysis and dysfunction. Whether pragmatism is revived in America or arises out of other parts of the world,[3] it offers a new order of maturity and pluralism on which the future world may well depend.

What, then, *is* pragmatism?

Pragmatism began rumbling in American culture in the late 19th century, with insights about: 1) the choices and responsibilities humans have in relation to the theories we adopt; 2) the practical consequences of those adoptions; and 3) the fact that we can never fully understand any theory until we see what it comes to in action. But the heart of it lies in an intensely personal crisis, and the struggle to live the expanded vision of human maturity this crisis mediates.

Pragmatism in its full and deep sense arises from encounter with the distinctly post-traditional experience of nihilism and Nothingness. Nihilism is the experience of ungroundedness, meaninglessness, and the reduction of all value to those of materiality, interest, and power. Nihilism is a widespread condition, especially in post-traditional circumstances, after the initial intoxication of modern life and its endless horizons of negative freedom have worn off;[4] after we have experienced the meaning of Janis Joplin's lament that "Freedom's just another word for nothing left to lose."[5] Many become stuck there, in "lives of quiet desperation," as well as in more active lives of resentful and cynical negativity, some even to the point of terrorism. The crazed wish to tear down, shoot down, or otherwise obliterate that which has so deeply disappointed and/or become unavailable demonstrates Nietzsche's point that "man [sic] would sooner have the void for his purpose than be void of purpose."[6] But some others are able to move beyond nihilism to the experience of Nothingness as the radically mysterious source of everything. It is at this point that we begin to experience what William James identified as that most profound religious experience of "new ranges of life succeeding on our most despairing moments."[7] Experience of Nothingness, as a radicalization of nihilism, opens beyond negation on to the ineffable, overflowing wellspring of life.

This is not a passive experience, since it is simultaneous with the decision and action of stepping beyond nihilism, with the conscious decision to affirm life as a gift.[8] This includes adopting an interpretation of life that articulates values, beliefs, and commitments, without any metaphysical certification as to their correctness. It acknowledges that our chosen interpretation inevitably reflects, at least in part, our local situation and limited capacities for symbolizing and articulation. Further, pragmatism also entails the will to ongoing growth and transformation, including, but not limited to, the willingness to modify or even replace the life interpretation we have adopted or created, according to its effectiveness in maintaining and deepening our life-affirmation. Clearly it takes a significant degree of development and maturity to even acknowledge pragmatism as a possibility.[9]

Pragmatism runs deep, even to the decision as to whether life is worth living, a decision on which terrorists and other nihilists have come down negatively. This is why understanding pragmatism requires going back to the root existential moment. William James, to take America's leading example of a post-traditional person who became a pragmatist, was overwhelmed by the forces of modern scientific determinism and its bleak personal implications. He was unable to find comfort in the cultural resources associated with traditional Greek and Hebrew senses of "God." He contemplated suicide as the most honest thing a serious person could do. Then, after many crises and bouts of deep depression, he somehow finally decided to "go a step further" to "posit life." He said: "My first act of free will shall be to believe in free will."[10] Then, through the rest of his career, he built pragmatism on the initially fragile footing of this decision and the realizations that followed from it. This included a most strange fact of life on this planet: that our "will[ing] to believe" is sometimes a prerequisite for that in which we believe (like love and justice and God) to be present and active in the world and in ourselves.[11] It is in this sense that he remarked, toward the end of his career, that "[p]hilosophies are intimate parts of the universe, they express something of its own thought of itself. A philosophy may indeed be a most momentous reaction of the universe upon itself."[12] Passively considered, the universe may be attempting to act through us; on the active side, it may be that our beliefs are somehow—beyond "social construction" in the usual sociological sense—actually constitutive of reality itself. We may be co-creators, or we may have good reasons for choosing to think of ourselves in this way.

This orientation, though, is challenging developmentally, especially against the backdrop of inherited Western assumptions about the relationship between belief and choice. Among the challenges is the fact that, since the *act* of choosing or willing to believe is prior to any particular belief that is chosen, it is impossible to get a metaphysic or a doctrine out of pragmatism. Metaphysics are taken seriously, but as choices—with consequences (an idea that is mind-bending from the perspective of traditional assumptions). What one chooses to believe needs to be understood not as proclamations of certain and certified correspondence with Reality itself, but as provisional hypotheses that offer hope and encouragement in their support of a more faithful way of living.

Because the positing of life is so entirely dependent on a developmental movement, including an intensely existential decision and its individualized consequences, pragmatism is difficult to communicate. It is not ideological, but neither is it relativistic; it is not a metaphysical claim, but neither is it ungrounded; it cannot be formulated, but it can be identified. This sounds a little like Daoism or Zen, and indeed it is, insofar as pragmatism points to a locus of vitality that is and must remain ineffable, requiring us to resist the human temptation of closure and control. Pragmatism is acutely aware of this temptation, and that succumbing to it results in obstruction of the reality to which it responds. This is the very definition of idolatry: worshipping the symbol rather than that to which it points. Pragmatism is progressively more refined faithfulness to the source of life; it is response to the gift that flows out of Nothingness, in radical distinction from the constriction and deflection of nihilism.

Pragmatism contains a strong injunction for humans to grow up and live with and *in* an aliveness and a maturity—including an acceptance of fragility and vulnerability—that has been rare in the human past. Further, the maturity envisioned by pragmatism is profoundly pluralistic and relational, which is to say, it is quite different from both traditional authoritarianism and tepid modern toleration, the latter with its negative, private, and relativistic freedom of live and let live. The pluralism inherent to pragmatism is the more vigorous pluralism of mutual growth, dialogue, and democracy, where democracy is understood in the way that Dewey famously defined it. Democracy, he wrote, is much more than a form of government: "it is primarily a mode of associated living, of conjoint, communicated experience."[13] It is a life-way in which our principles and commitments very much matter, yet do not need to be absolutized. Contradictory though it may sound at first, all one must do to enter the creative space of this pluralism is to acknowledge the limitations of our articulation and to affirm the possibility that we might grow through the insights and presence of others who are different from ourselves. Pragmatism provides a profoundly positive response to the challenge of alterity that marks our era.

Pragmatism is post-traditional in that it arises as an intuition and a way of living before it becomes a "philosophy." It arises out of a sense of the failure, misdirection, or insufficiency of those traditional ways of interpretation we inherit. In the West, this sense is strongly associated with the problem of intellectualism, precisely the ideological life orientation we suffer from today, arising from the tendency of Western people to withdraw from the immediacy of lived life into static and closed conceptual systems. These systems then wind up constraining rather than supporting life, doing violence to life in the name of conceptual order and control. After two millennia of traditional abstraction from life, pragmatism is centered on *return*—to value and meaning located in the deep textures of life itself. It answers a question that has lain dormant in Plato for many centuries, namely the question as to why—apart from compulsion—the enlightened being would return to live in the cave-like darkness of the world. Pragmatism acknowledges it may be necessary to withdraw attention from the urgency of life on the surface in order to develop the capacities of reason, reflection, self-transcendence, and purpose, but this is not sufficient for human development. The necessary functions of abstraction come to healthy fulfillment not by remaining in the detachment of Mount Olympus, but rather by going the step further to return to the ever changing, ever-ambiguous, ever-struggling world. Here we interact with others in the pluralistic space of democratic problem-solving, discovery, and growth, with others who may have come to different conclusions about the matters at hand, and who just may have seen more clearly than we ourselves on some issues. The philosopher king [sic] returns because life in the world is the greater challenge and adventure, the greater life-affirmation.

Pragmatism understands that the spirit or energy we need in life as source of guidance, motivation, and healthy growth, comes not from obedience to command from on high, and/or "correspondence" of our lives with a displaced and static metaphysical order outside of the world. It comes from the depth of connection with a continuous flow of gift-full energy that is already present in our lives and the world, if only we would learn to be alert and responsive to its presence. Pragmatism, then, as a philosophy of return, does not reject the human need for abstraction, principle, and moral/political direction. Rather, it evaluates these by their fruits in relation to consequences *in life*, ever mindful that the old Western dream of achieving a single, final set of absolutized abstractions has been outgrown and rendered dangerous.[14]

In pragmatism's effort to live ever more fully in and through direct contact with the deepest and utterly ineffable wellspring of life, it assumes that human beings are capable of this. Each person, each in their unique way, is capable of bearing the goodness of life directly into the world, independent of mediating hierarchies. This happens with ever greater purity and intensity through the process of transformation, which is the underlying drama of human life first identified by the traditions that arose in the Axial Age (roughly 900–200 BCE).[15] The utterly crucial decision to live in a life-affirming way may occur first in some dramatic moment, as with James, in an awakening, conversion, or *metanoia* experience. But it also occurs repeatedly and with ever greater refinement as we grow and mature in our capacity to be faithful to life—in never-ending cycles of self-transcendence or self-overcoming—until we approach the point where we are able to embody it in pure form, unpolluted by ego. This ideal end of the transformative process we see, for example, in Chinese *wu wei* (the action of non-action), Christian proclamation "it is no longer I who live, but Christ who lives in me" (Galatians 2:20), Socratic "knowing nothing," Hindu exclamation "Atman is Brahman"—and in William James' essential though illusive term, "pure experience."[16]

Between now and full embodiment of that ideal, though, we will necessarily and inevitably have a "philosophy" as our life-interpretation. It serves, whether we recognize it explicitly or not, to provide direction in the transformation process. But no philosophy is perfect, nor is the one that is appropriate to you necessarily the one that is most effective for me at this point in my own journey. Actually, from the standpoint of the ideal just stated, the very fact of our having a philosophy at all is testimony to our incompleteness. So we need to be especially careful, again, not to freeze our philosophies into static and absolutized positions. It is essential to remember that the lure of certainty—what James called "the queerest idol ever invented in the philosophic cave"[17]—is profoundly self and life defeating.[18] Our philosophies must be understood not as perfect reflections of a reality that is outside of and prior to life, but rather as approximations and aids to our growth. In the maturity that is integral to pragmatism, we do well to keep in mind Karl Jaspers' definition of philosophy as "the thought with which or as which I am active as my own self,"[19] where "active" is a synonym for the ideal of living pure affirmation.

Actually, this radically alternative way of philosophy, this way of holding the intellect and letting it support the living of a life, harkens back to Socrates, before he was eclipsed by the intellectualism that followed and dominated in the West after Plato and Aristotle. In both Socrates and pragmatism, the ways we think and what we think cannot be derived from strictly propositional logic; matters of heart and soul must be involved as well. Socrates spoke of philosophies as "magic spells" we sing over the frightened child within "until you have charmed away his fears," and as accounts we use "to inspire ourselves" in the transformative process of purifying the soul.[20] It is important to note that this more practical and intuitive orientation to philosophy is making a comeback in Western culture today not only through pragmatism, but also through the contemplative mind movement which distinguishes contemplation as an epistemology that reaches deeper than the rationalism and empiricism that have been dominant in Western culture for so many centuries.[21] Socrates referred to the contemplative dimension in terms of "knowing nothing"; James spoke of it as "the gospel of relaxation."[22]

Philosophies, then, need to be evaluated and continuously refined from the perspective of their consequences for growth and creativity, for justice and sustainability, for their responsiveness to the ever-emerging possibilities and dangers of lived life, and for their capacity to contribute to a world that is more like gift and less like constraint. Here is an answer to the question often put to pragmatism: "Consequences for what? Why isn't pragmatism just a free-floating method, another form of instrumentalism, or the same old Western individualism?" Pragmatism answers by saying that under post-traditional circumstances *the principle of life affirmation* is sufficient as both ideal and guidance in life. Philosophies can and should be assessed in terms of their capacity to support us in living through progressively more direct contact with the source of life. This understanding is rigorous and respectful of the work of the intellect and the wisdom of traditions. It also includes emotion and the dimension of care, relationality, and embodiment, with the latter as that moment in life when universality and particularity come to simultaneity. Pragmatism moves beyond the Cartesian mind-body dichotomy by embracing both in the spirit of our life-affirmation.

However, pragmatism claims no special access to the maturity it cultivates. Rather, it affirms, in the best sense of American "religious freedom," the capacity of many traditions to facilitate and guide the transformative process, according to the needs of particular people in particular social-cultural-personal circumstances. Hence pragmatism is more a way of *holding* a theory than it is ideological subscription to any particular theory in the traditional sense. James speaks of this in terms of the geniality of pragmatism:

> she 'unstiffens' our theories. She has in fact no prejudices whatsoever, no obstructive dogmas, no rigid canons of what shall count as proof. She is completely genial. She will

entertain any hypothesis, she will consider any evidence... Her manners are as various and flexible, her resources as rich and various, and her conclusions as friendly as those of mother nature.[23]

It is in this way that pragmatism also can be spoken of as distinctly post-traditional, as a tradition beyond traditions, and as pluralistic in essence. Pragmatism simultaneously affirms both our differences and our deep commonality in what James calls "the common mother," our Earthbound condition, and our shared wish to live a life of "sympathy" rather than "cynicism."[24]

Returning to the themes with which this essay began, pragmatism presents a way beyond both the unending ideological standoff of public life and the forms of private life that generate moral disease. It leads to a dynamic pluralism in which we no longer need to convert one another but to communicate and appreciate, to see what the other sees. It leads to a pluralism that is sufficiently attractive that it can call us off our soapboxes and out of our private obsessions, into the clear air of democratic encounter. Pragmatism opens onto that vision of democracy that led Walt Whitman famously to remark that "it is a word the real gist of which still sleeps... [Its] history has yet to be enacted."[25]

Think of it in terms of how new energy enters into the world and ourselves. In both ideology and privatism we become isolated, subject to the entropy of being closed off from the energies to which we have access when we are fully ourselves in the presence of each other. Indeed, the condition of isolation seems to describe how empires collapse and how individuals become unhealthy, both lonely and incapable of solitude.[26] They become alienated from the kind of relationship—call it democratic, dialogical, compassionate, or deep pluralism—through which new energy flows into and through our lives and the lives we share with others.[27] The inner secret of the great traditions available to us in our times—precisely when so many could care less—is that the locus of full human development is not mystical detachment from the messiness of the world, but rather in the space of return, in compassionate engagement. Karen Armstrong, speaking of that Axial Age in which the great traditions shared a common origin, goes so far as to say that at the center of the traditions "religion *was* compassion," and that our most urgent need today is to "go in search of the lost heart, the spirit of compassion that lies at the core of all of our traditions."[28]

Perhaps the most tragic aspect of the modern scientific and individualistic paradigm is that it limits possibility in any but the physical dimension, where its accomplishments are so dazzling that many fail to notice its moral and spiritual poverty. Addition, subtraction, and rearrangement can occur, but not qualitative change or increase, nothing like real transformation or growth.[29] The modern paradigm is so tightly wound in its obsession with order, control, and materiality, and so satisfied with the efficacy of its manipulation of both the natural world and other persons, that it leaves no space for fresh energy, or quality, or emergent truth. A certain starvation sets in; at the same time, there arise more and more severe attempts to order life through rationality alone. The modern repression and sublimation of vital life-energy into the service of modernity's mechanical purposes was, of course, the secret to its Faustian success. But as this orientation turns in on itself, suffocates, and breaks down, we are also learning that it is lethal. The modern paradigm is, in a word, unsustainable.

The pragmatic sensibility can help us turn away from what has happened repeatedly in human history, as civilizations poison themselves with the arrogance of their successes and the obsolescence of their underlying strategies. Against this decadence, pragmatism can help us position ourselves in such a way that our differences can open onto a deeper commonality in the wellspring through which life is sustained and renewed — what John Dewey called "the great community."[30] For it is in the democratic relationship — which is as inherent to pragmatism as contemplative "relaxation"[31] — that we can re-establish contact with both ourselves and others. In this way we conceive of new strategies suitable to what Tu Weiming, one of the great world citizens of our era, distinguishes as a *learning* civilization rather than a teaching civilization.[32]

It may be too late for America to wake up and revive through rising to the maturity that is the essence of pragmatism. But it is clearly not too late for the life-affirming voice of American pragmatism to join and enrich the global movement from teaching to learning, from monologue to dialogue, from domination to pluralism.[33] And if there were to be a reappropriation of pragmatism in America, one key to its occurring might be found in a remark by Amartya Sen about the attitudes of many Americans toward democracy in its global context. He observed that many fail to support democracy in other parts of the world for fear of imposing "Western ideas of democracy." The assumption behind this attitude, one that manages to be both arrogant and self-deprecating at the same time, is that democracy is "an immaculate Western conception," as distinct from an aspiration with "global roots."[34] In like fashion, we would do well to be aware that pragmatism, too, has global roots. It also has practical value — as a way of thinking and thinking about thinking — in the developmental movement from post-traditional confusion into a new order of maturity in which unity and diversity are not opposed, and in which thriving might occur despite improbability.

ENDNOTES

1   Wallace Stevens, "The Well Dressed Man with a Beard," in *The Palm at the End of the Mind,* ed. Holly Stevens (New York: Vintage Books, 1972), 190.

2   On these qualities, as well as on what I take to be the authentic underlying attitude of pragmatism, see Dwayne Tunstall and his "Cornell West, John Dewey, and the Tragicomic Undercurrents of Deweyan Creative Democracy," *Contemporary Pragmatism* 5, 2 (December 2008): 109–29.

3   From Singapore, for example, see the work of Sor-hoon Tan. For the story of how John Dewey's presence in China (1919–1921) led

a considerable number of influential Chinese people to identify themselves as pragmatists, see Jessica Ching-Sze Wang, *John Dewey in China: To Teach and To Learn* (Albany: SUNY Press, 2007).

4   For extended discussion of nihilism and modern life, see my *Overcoming America/America Overcoming* (Lanham, MD: Lexington Books, 2013).

5   Kris Kristofferson, "Me and Bobby McGee," song lyrics, 1970.

6   Friedrich Nietzsche, *The Genealogy of Morals,* in Francis Golffing, trans., ed., *The Birth of Tragedy and the Genealogy of Morals* (Garden City, NJ: Doubleday Anchor, 1956), 299.

7   William James, "Conclusions" *[to A Pluralistic Universe],* as "[An Overview]" in John J. McDermott, ed., *The Writings of William James* (Chicago: University of Chicago Press, 1977), 800–01.

8   On the cultural and philosophical implications of thinking in terms of gift, see Calvin O. Schrag, *God as Otherwise Than Being: Toward a Semantics of the Gift* (Evanston, IL: Northwestern University Press, 2002).

9   I speak of the relationship between pragmatism and human development insofar as they both involve the actualization of higher order cognitive function. See the works of Benjamin Bloom, Carol Gilligan, Lawrence Kohlberg, and William Perry.

10 From a journal entry dated April 30, 1870, in *The Writings of William James,* 7–8.

11 James, "The Will to Believe," in *Writings,* 731.

12 James, "Conclusions," in *Writings,* 805.

13 John Dewey, *Experience and Education* (New York: Macmillan, 1938), 87.

14 For a brilliant discussion of the limitations and dangers of this dream, see Mary Midgley, "Sustainability and Moral Pluralism," in Victoria Davion, ed. *Ethics and the Environment* (Greenwich, CT: JAI, 1966), 41–54.

15 A root source of this understanding is Karl Jaspers' *The Origin and Goal of History* (New Haven: Yale University Press, 1953). A recent strong statement of the Axial thesis is Karen Armstrong's *The Great*

Transformation: The Beginning of Our Religious Traditions (New York: Alfred A. Knopf, 2006). Aldous Huxley, Huston Smith, John Hick, and Jacob Needleman, among others, elaborate on this understanding of transformation as deep commonality among the traditions.

16 James, "A World of Pure Experience," in *The Writings of William James*, 194–214.

17 James, "The Will to Believe," in *The Writings of William James*, 734.

18 On fallibilism as inherent to pragmatism, see the work of Richard J. Bernstein, especially *The Pragmatic Turn* (Malden, MA: Polity Press, 2010).

19 Karl Jaspers, *Man in the Modern Age,* Eden and Cedar Paul, trans. (Garden City, NJ: Anchor Books, 1957), 198.

20 Plato, *Phaedo* 77e, 114d, in the *Collected Dialogues of Plato,* eds. Edith Hamilton and Huntington Cairns (New York: Pantheon Books, 1985), 61, 95.

21 See Tobin Hart, "Opening the Contemplative Mind in the Classroom," in *Journal of Transformative Education* 2.1 (January 2004): 28–46. See also the Center for Contemplative Mind in Society at http://www.contemplativemind.org/.

22 William James, "The Gospel of Relaxation," in *Talks to Teachers on Psychology: and to Students on Some of Life's Ideals* (New York: Norton, 1958), 132–48. For James and others, for example, Paul Tillich, another significant occasion of contemplative knowing is what James identified as the most profound religious experience of "new ranges of life arising out of our most despairing moments." See James, "A Pluralistic Universe," in *Essays in Radical Empiricism and a Pluralistic Universe,* ed. Richard J. Bernstein (New York: Dutton, 1971), 265–66.

23 James, "What Pragmatism Means," in *The Writings of William James*, 389–90.

24 James, "The Types of Philosophic Thinking," in *The Writings of William James*, 486, 489.

25 Walt Whitman, *Democratic Vistas,* ed. Ed Folsom (Iowa City: University of Iowa Press, 2010), 37.

26 On the crucial distinction between loneliness and solitude, see

Hannah Arendt, *The Life of the Mind* (San Diego: Harcourt Harvest, 1978), 185.

27 On this theme in pragmatism, see the work of Judith M. Green, especially *Pragmatism and Social Hope* (New York: Columbia University Press, 2008).

28 Armstrong, *The Great Transformation,* xiii, 399.

29 See my "The Adulthood We Need: Education and Developmental Challenge in the US and China," in Judy Whipps, ed. *Reflect, Connect, Engage: Liberal Education at GVSU* (Acton, MA: XanEdu Press, 2013), 400–13, and Jal Mehta, *The Allure of Order: High Hopes, Dashed Expectations, and the Troubled Quest to Remake American Schooling* (Oxford: Oxford University Press, 2013).

30 John Dewey, "The Search for the Great Community," in *The Public and Its Problems* (Chicago: Swallow Press, 1927), 143–84.

31 James Luther Adams, one of the great relational or democratic liberals of the 20th century, commenting on the collapse of liberal/progressive politics by 1968, explicitly counted lack of "disciplines of the inner life" and "neglect [of] the deeper levels of both the human consciousness and of reality itself" as major factors. See my "Toward a Postliberal Liberalism: James Luther Adams and the Need for a Theory of Relational Meaning," in *American Journal of Philosophy and Theology* 17.1 (January 1996): 51–70.

32 Tu Weiming, "Implications of the Rise of 'Confucian' East Asia," *Daedalus: Journal of the American Academy of Arts and Sciences* 129.1 (Winter 2000): 209.

33 An excellent example of this joining and enriching through pragmatism is found in the work of Singapore scholar Sor-hoon Tan, especially in her book, *Confucian Democracy: A Deweyan Reconstruction* (Albany: SUNY Press, 2003). Another fine example is Steve Odin, *The Social Self in Zen and American Pragmatism* (Albany: SUNY Press, 1996).

34 Amartya Sen, "Democracy and Its Global Roots," in *The New Republic,* 6 October 2003, 35.

10

THROUGH AND BEYOND

A Contemporary Soteriology

THE NEW WORLDVIEW SO URGENTLY NEEDED on our planet is actually already emerging in our midst. It is arising through our experience, though it is difficult to find confirmation in this, even within ourselves. We don't have the space in our multitasking lives to honor or cultivate that deeper dimension of our lives in which the new worldview is active. Neither do we have the language or structures of interpretation by which to identify and maintain focus on what is most compelling in our experience. But still, most of us catch glimpses of it from time to time. We see it in moments of cross-cultural friendship, expanded senses of possibility, and awareness that our lives and the Earth itself are gifts in the midst of Nothingness.

WORLDVIEW, EXPERIENCE, AND INTERPRETATION

If we are to avoid a fate like that of lemmings driving themselves over the cliff of oblivion, a fate to which the human race is already well-invested, we must find a way to reconnect with ourselves and the ways in which we are bearers of something much deeper than what the older, passing worldview allows us to conceive of as "self."[1] We need to wake up to the dignity of a species-nature more compassionate and appreciative than that of our ancestors.

There are actually quite a few groups and figures out there that are available to help us in this calling to embody a new worldview. But there is a problem with much of the "help" that becomes available, as indicated by Whitehead's comment that "great ideas enter into reality with evil associates and with disgusting alliances."[2] In times like ours, it is excruciatingly difficult to distinguish real help from the tricks of charlatans and exploiters.[3] This is the case even though, as Whitehead went on to say, "the greatness remains, nerving the race in its slow ascent."[4] The temptation is to just give up, to live a life of quiet resignation to the sad conclusion that personal gain is the only thing we can hope for.

One kind of resource that helps greatly in the choices we must make is *interpretation*, and that is what I seek to provide in this writing. There is a discernible developmental pathway that leads through the confusions and dangers of the late modern and postmodern periods in which we live. It moves in the direction of a new ethic and spirituality, and the new worldview of which I speak. For starters, we can say that this new worldview is quite distinct from the old one that colonized the planet in the Enlightenment era. That worldview centered on the Western vision of universality achieved through retreat from the body of actual life, into both abstracted rationality and isolated individualism. The most immediate contrast between the old and new worldviews is that the new one is relational to the core and capable of living in and through the radiant paradox of embodied life on Earth. This is the paradox of something-nothing, of many-one, of diversity-unity. Finally, we are beginning to get past the old either-or ways of dichotomous thinking that come grinding to ideological standoff and contradiction in our time.

But this is jumping ahead, so it might sound strange. Since the new worldview is a way of living, not a static philosophical formulation or doctrine, it needs to be articulated through a stream of experience that is widely shared among people living today. It needs to be experienced as movement through a cultural and spiritual morass into a much better place, a healthier and more fulfilling way to live than had been permitted in the past. But, again, this stream of experience has not yet been well articulated, such that people have access to an overall understanding that supports and guides them in the momentous choices required on the way to and within this new worldview. That, then, is the purpose of this essay: to provide interpretations of some broadly shared experiences of positive movement along a developmental pathway, crossing over a fundamental threshold, and moving into a new era in which the challenge is to embody a new and ever dynamic worldview.

MODERN, POSTMODERN, AND BEYOND

Beginning in 17th century Europe, the modern period achieved much of its definition through opposition to medieval religion, especially its supernaturalism and authoritarianism. As it progressed, modernity became increasingly secular, scientific, and individualistic. There emerged a certain catholicity of scientific rationality, joined with natural rights individualism as the dominating worldview, which suppressed and choked out virtually all other ways of responding to the mystery of life on this planet. The values associated with this modern catholicity were the negative "natural rights" of individual autonomy, competition, materialism (or "property" in Locke's statement of them), consumption, and the myth of "automatic harmony" as the imagined result of everyone pursuing their interests.[5] These rights were declared to be universal, but in fact were available only to elites. Modernity triumphed over tradition through its joining of science and individualism.

Then, by the late 20th century, after almost four centuries of the contagious spread of modernity across the planet, strong protest to this worldview began to appear in various parts of the world, in what came to be called a "post-secular era."⁶ It was as though the human spirit—in alignment with Earth itself—was protesting against the insufficiency of modern values, including the imposition of those values both explicitly and implicitly across the globe, through a hypnotic sort of imperialism.⁷ A wide variety of movements appeared, from those attempting to reclaim a spirituality distinct from religion, to those fundamentalist groups wanting a return to "traditional" religion. And there was terrorism: the fanatical wish to simply destroy the modern edifice.

Many of those who were able to avoid these more extreme responses developed a new appreciation for those traditions that had been so hastily rejected in the rush to modernity. Along with this appreciation there also emerged an understanding of commonality among the historic traditions. The "perennial philosophy" idea, championed in the mid-to-later 20th century by Aldous Huxley, Joseph Campbell, Karl Jaspers, Hannah Arendt, and Huston Smith, affirmed a deep yet paradoxically diverse commonality among peoples of traditional cultures. Their reach for meaning and value beyond the limited vision of modernity, for a state of enlightenment, salvation, or maturity, appeared to be remarkably similar across the nearly forgotten traditions. This understanding was mostly articulated in terms of shared beliefs and metaphysics, myths, symbols, and archetypes.

The new experience of universality represented a rediscovery of the sacred, a rediscovery of the possibility of connection with an order of reality that is both beyond the ordinary and, at the same time, most intimate with ordinary, individual existence; an order overflowing with meaning, value, and possibility. This experience involved the awakening of a basic human longing. It served to illuminate, by contrast, the limitations of the modern worldview based on the universalizing of science and individuality, and the corresponding orientation of shallow materialism, hypocrisy, and an unhappy mix of conformism and isolation. Protest and rejection of modernity followed, movements of counter-culture critique, and attempts to inhabit a life-way far deeper and richer than that of mainline Western society.

But by the late 20th century, disappointment with the discovery of a perennial philosophy also began to surface: disappointment with the fact that, in the midst of often energetic appreciation of the "many ways up the mountain," few were actually engaged in the practices through which any real movement or development might occur. The new perception of universality turned out to be more aesthetic than religious; it was limited to appreciation and protest, unable to actually move toward that state of enlightenment or salvation it envisioned. The perennialist perch offered an excellent view, but it did not facilitate travel. It turned out to be the Western romanticism all over again.

For some, disappointment resulted in retreat back into the modern life-way they had earlier rejected, but with a certain nihilistic cynicism that further contributed to the moral disease of postmodern society. Those who withstood the frustrations that followed awareness of the limitations of the new universality came upon yet another discovery, now in the form of a paradox: humans need particularity in order to get to the genuine experience of universality or the sacred—enlightenment, or salvation—that we cherish. Without commitment and humble, persistent practice within an inevitably limited and imperfect particularity, there is no experience of universality as anything more than the momentary "high" that can as well be provided by a movie theater, tourism, or drugs.

Discovery and growth continued, now in the form of the realization that the deep commonality among the world's great traditions is not that of agreement about metaphysics or shared belief, but rather of transformative practice. What the great traditions of the Axial Age were fundamentally about was facilitation of the developmental movement from beings driven by ego (or *karma,* or sin—there are many descriptions of the initial condition of self-concern and control as expressions of profound alienation and fear) to beings who are tuned to an infinitely deeper and more reliable source of direction in life.[8] The language, metaphysical claims, and other cultural supports of traditional culture were just that—supports for movement to a way of life that cannot ever be captured and contained in ordinary discursive language. In fact, the all too human urge to capture and contain is the very definition, in Western terms, of idolatry: worshipping the symbol rather than that toward which it points. This recalling of the radical ineffability of the ultimate in life, and the radically limited nature of our religious and cultural symbolizing, has led many to fresh understanding of such Axial Age documents as Lao Tsu's *Dao De Jing,* beginning with: "The Dao that can be spoken is not the eternal Dao."

Here we need to pause on the pathway we are following. We need to take note of the enormous challenges these discoveries, and this last one in particular, present for Western people, the ways they can attract "disgusting alliances," or, in the terms of Robert N. Bellah's description of the same developmental territory we are traversing here, "possibilities of pathological distortion."[9] For our cultural heritage—in our religion, philosophy, and science—is one of finding orientation in life by reference to a single, detached, and static metaphysic, a vision of "out there" that stabilizes and supervises what is happening "down here." The implication of the discovery that any interpretation is at least partially a product of the particularity out of which it arises, and that no metaphysic can be completely right is profoundly unsettling to the Western mind. In fact, it frequently provokes collapse into relativism and/or nihilism. The hermeneutical revolution of the 20th century, with its acute awareness of the limited and "socially constructed" nature of any cultural commitment beyond individual interest and power, has taken a long time to digest. That revolution has been unable to solve the riddle Socrates presented when he said it is necessary to "risk the belief" that the soul exists as that dimension of ourselves that is confluent with the Good; or when

William James suggests that this risk may be the most essential human action; and when Confucius says "It is not the Way that makes the human great, but the human that makes the Way great"[10]—that the Way requires collaboration with humans in order to be present and effective on this planet. A metaphysic may be necessary in order to support human transformation, but it needs to be held in a way that is very different from how Western ancestors wielded their beliefs in the past. Westerners need to move beyond the post-traditional antinomy between absolutized foundationalisms and nihilistic relativism.

Now back on the path: The earlier universalism of appreciation foundered on two issues: 1) appreciation abstracted from practice proved to be insufficient; and 2) a universalism that could encompass the human need for particularity seemed impossible, or totally arbitrary, as though any particularity would do as well as any other. Perhaps we were provided with initial glimpses of a new universality in an interim stage of appreciation in order to motivate us to keep moving on the path. And move we must, because at some point we come to the disjunction between appreciative awareness of transformation and actual engagement. We need to make some difficult choices as to a particular commitment and a way of actual practice. This is an extremely uncomfortable threshold. Knowing the inevitable limitations of any actual commitment, especially when compared with the purity of potential and the beauty of detached universality, we also become aware of the dangers of fundamentalism, cults, and the consequences of unfortunate choice. And we realize that we are really not qualified to direct our own practice, at the same time we are unsure as to who we can trust. And, in addition to all of the above, we live in a society of endless distraction where the kind of focus required for good choice and solid practice seems both impossible and perhaps even impermissible. It's as though it might be better to simply ignore those deeper messages mentioned at the beginning of this essay and slip into the mere persistence of the consumer life.

Despite all of the above, at some point there is no way to avoid the need to commit to a particular form of practice (or, in some cases, to acknowledge that we have already done so, for better or for worse), no matter how humble our beginning might be. The other choice (of not choosing) is a descent into non-thriving and generalized retreat from life. I think at this point about the decision to confront an addiction. Here, too, is movement across a threshold that is very small and simple in one way, and yet utterly vast in another. Here, too, we find ourselves needing to override the ego, including its capacity to seize the rational mind and construct all kinds of reasons as to why today is not the day. Finally, it comes down to that most basic advice of our era that is captured so strangely well in the Nike commercial: "Just do it." Simple, but not easy.

In the stepping across, onto a more or less reliable structure of particularity, we simultaneously engage the utterly crucial act of affirming life against the backdrop of Nothingness or the abyss, beyond nihilism, in the absence of any traditional metaphysical or cultural support — as an "absurd" act of positive response to the gift quality of life. Perhaps a more effective way to describe this utterly crucial act is found not in traditional mysticism, but in contemporary social science. An example is William Perry's social scientific description of healthy college life as a developmental movement from Absolutism, through Relativism, and into the mature phase he refers to as "Commitment." He says that the Commitment phase centers on "an affirmation made in a world perceived as relativistic, that is *after* detachment, doubt, and awareness of alternatives have made the experience of personal choice a possibility," and where choice "require[s] the courage of responsibility, and presuppose[s] an acceptance of human limits, including the limits of reason."[11]

But this interpretation I am weaving is just too abstract! What *really* motivates and sustains in the choice of a particular practice and the process of its ongoing refinement is actual *experience of coincidence between universal and particular dimensions* of life on this planet:

those experiences of the universal that are completely simultaneous with particularity, and those moments of luminous particularity that coincide with eternity.[12] These fundamentally religious experiences are a "natural" part of human life, a fact that is recognized in all of the great traditions, though one that has not been much celebrated or cultivated in the modern era of science and individualism, with their preference for abstracted knowledge, isolated personhood, and the push-pull world of Newtonian physics and social contract. In those moments when simultaneity actually occurs, moments sometimes referred to as "presence," or "embodiment," or of dwelling in what we might call the "sweet spot" of life on this planet, we participate in the radiant, life-giving paradox of the sacred on Earth. Though we often alienate ourselves from this experience through interpretations that misplace or displace it, it is our deepest longing and an experience that resonates with and awakens our authentic nature.

Of course, the best way to recognize this coincidence is from within our chosen practice, and to understand that in a very real way this *is* our practice: dwelling in the paradoxical simultaneity of particular and universal dimensions, first in a very specific and carefully demarcated activity, and then, if all goes well, progressively throughout the whole of our life. In fact, this is how to know whether our chosen practice is authentic and effective, if it 1) is punctuated with occasional moments of simultaneity, and if 2) this way of being penetrates and transforms our ordinary presence in the world.[13]

But, as with the Dao in Lao Tsu's statement, these moments cannot be grasped. We cannot own them, capture or contain them, or sustain them—at least not initially. At best, they come and go. And in the meanwhile we continue to work, to refine and develop. We continue to grow. We do this through an oscillating movement back and forth, between phases of isolated and near incommensurable particularity, and phases of universality in which we and our practice are almost completely dissolved in *what is*. It is essential to accept without disappointment or distraction that this oscillation is integral to spiritual life, some part of which is acceptance of the inevitability of distraction, disappointment, and even despair.[14]

The experience of meditation, contemplation, or mystical prayer, which is taken as central to—though not exhaustive of—spiritual formation in most traditions, provides invaluable experiential insight into the nature of this vital oscillation. The practice itself dwells in paradox: "thinking nothing," and at the same time focusing on a mantra (one's breath, a three-to-five syllable phrase, a physical object—something very specific and immediate on which to focus one's attention.[15]) Just think nothing, be radically open, sit in complete ineffability. When distracting thoughts or emotions interrupt and carry attention away, as they inevitably will, gently move to the mantra as the center of particularity and focus. Then let focus give way to thinking nothing, let simultaneity between particularity and total openness occur. Gradually (or sometimes more immediately, as in the sudden realization of Zen *Satori, Ah this!*), learn to sustain this form of meditation as the way of living we have come to call "mindfulness."[16]

Here we should pause again to take note of one other major inhibition, especially for Western people, one that exists right alongside and at least initially as the opposite of the previously discussed reluctance of commitment to particularity. The second kind of inhibition is acute shyness about any kind of generalizing, universalizing, or "essentializing." This shyness is borne out of the fear that generalizing of any kind will replicate the hegemonic universalizing of the Western past, the universalizing in terms of abstract, ahistorical, transcendent principles known and mediated through either reason or divine command and the earthly structures of hierarchy they construct. This *kind* of universalizing, which is closely associated with the Western dependence on an absolutized metaphysic, legitimated imperialism of all kinds, along with insensitivity and real blindness to the dynamics of life at all levels, all the while operating under the illusion of superiority and control. But there is literally a world of difference between this orientation and the universalizing through depth I am describing, what some have called "situated universalism."[17] Within this newer (to the West) universalizing, it becomes possible to solve one of the most basic riddles of our era: how to affirm similarity and difference simultaneously, unity and diversity, the one and the many—how the magnificent though heretofore mysterious American ideal of *E pluribus unum* becomes a real possibility.

We should also note that shyness about universalizing is not necessarily passive or benign. It can actually be dangerous. A statement from Amartya Sen presents the danger with great clarity in relation to a certain reticence about democracy:

> The apparent Western modesty that takes the form of a humble reluctance to promote 'Western ideas of democracy' in the non-Western world includes an imperious appropriation of a global heritage as exclusively the West's own. The self-doubt with regard to 'pushing' Western ideas on non-Western societies is combined with the absence of doubt in viewing democracy as a quintessentially Western idea, an immaculate Western conception.[18]

Sen is saying that shyness about universalizing can actually lead to a new and unconscious form of universalizing that is potentially even more pernicious than the old form. Another expression of this same problem is found in what Sor-hoon Tan calls "anti-democratic culturalism," the relativistic policy of non-intervention, which refuses to protest obvious cases of oppression and atrocity by invoking a conception of "culture" as a fixed body of norms and practices that "almost invariably [become] reductionist, essentialist, static, and hegemonic."[19] Again, fear of universalizing, and/or seeking exemption from the inevitability of universalizing, results in bad universalizing.

OSCILLATION AND EMERGENCE

Back again to the main pathway of developmental experience, movement within the vital oscillation between universality and particularity occurs through the opening up of three capacities that are central to the new worldview emerging in our time: dialogue, globalization, and compassion. This is not to imply that these capacities are entirely new to human experience, but rather that with movement across the developmental threshold of our era they come into a different field-ground relationship with other capacities. They come to stand out, while old capacities and values that had figured in the modern period—individualization, competition, defense against vulnerability—slip back into the shade. These are not gone, and they represent aspects of our humanity that need to continue functioning in healthy ways, but they no longer need to constitute the primary praxis of living a life.[20]

By way of extending description of movement beyond the morass of the modern and into a new maturity, spirituality, and worldview, let me say a little about each of the three emerging capacities.

Dialogue

Dialogue is the practice through which we mature into the ability to affirm similarity and difference simultaneously, learning to live and thrive in the complexity and ambiguity of relationship, stepping beyond the need for shelter in the closed simplicity of intellectual resolution of all questions. It is learning, as Rainer Maria Rilke famously said, to "live the questions." Dialogue is that relationship—sometimes called "democracy" in its thick or substantive form—in which we discover ourselves being more fully present in our authenticity with the other than in the isolation and exchange of natural rights individualism. It is the capacity through which we can tolerate and thrive in the realization that every human particularity universalizes and every universalization can be reduced to the particularity of its origin; we can experience more deeply what we have in common through learning about our differences—in what Hannah Arendt referred to as "the paradoxical plurality of beings who are all the same in that we are different."[21]

Hence we can hold our life interpretation—the "philosophy" or religious particularity—that supports our transformative practice in a different way, no longer needing to absolutize, and being open to ongoing refinement in the interpretive function as development occurs. Growth, rather than defense of The One Correct Way, becomes possible, and we learn that growth occurs most effectively through encounter with the other. In fact, we discover that in a very real way this encounter with the other *becomes* the "meditation" or core practice—as, for example, in the Christian "love thy neighbor as thyself," or the Confucian "human-hearted persons establish others if they want to establish themselves."[22]

Globalization

The term is awkward. The point is the emergence of a more global form of humanity, one that is distinct from the cosmopolitan aspirations of modernity, with its urge to reduce all to its own singular and constrained definition of the human. In dialogue we break through this false and reduced universality of the modern to encounter the other as Other—and the profound mystery of the world. We listen and see with a newly opened mind, are informed by others in ways that were not possible in our defensive-aggressive past, and in and through the encounter discover fresh access to the integrity of our own tradition and practice.

With globalization we go "beyond dialogue"[23] to expand our base of practice and responsiveness by selectively appropriating the insights of traditions other than our own. Globalization indicates the developed capacity to live in and through the genuine pluralism of dialogue—or, again, truly democratic relationship. It also indicates a new order of growth in which the spiritual and cultural riches of the world become available to persons for whom the resources of their own tradition are either incomplete, insufficient, not adequately tuned to their particular needs, or not completely manifest except when they are in the presence of other traditions. It indicates the developed capacity to draw on the riches of two or more of the world's traditions. The incredible new order of availability in our era has the potential to be overwhelming and confusing, as well as permitting superficial commodifications and cooptations of the world's great traditions, as in Whitehead's "disgusting alliances" mentioned above. But it also opens unprecedented possibilities for growth and acceleration of the transformation that is so urgently needed.

With globalization we become able to "cultivate a global memory,"[24] which will have the effect of blurring the sharp lines of distinction between traditions and result in new, interesting, and helpful combinations of traditions. Masao Abe, the great Zen teacher, has even suggested that this movement can result in a new universalism in which—speaking very broadly—the ontological depth of the East and the axiological acuteness of the West will cross-fertilize each other.[25] But again, this movement must be protected from the degradations just mentioned, including simple intellectualization. Huston Smith, with his assimilation of elements of Christianity, Hinduism, and Islam, is an excellent example of authentic appropriation of resources on a global scale.[26]

One very helpful way of evaluating the emergence of genuine globalization as distinct from mere homogenization and commodified surrogates of global humanity is the *consequences* for individual life and relationships. Does the movement in which one is traveling result in more of the superficial, multiple-tasking numbness and scattered attention that is so prevalent today, or does it result in what Peter Hershock suggestively describes as the "virtuosity" of "truly liberating intimacy," that is,

> a new kind of intimacy. Pursued in the spirit of expressing a truly liberating character—a character constituted not by the drawing of clear and controlled boundaries, but rather their erasure... Virtuosity is a trail we blaze only at high risk, by opening ourselves to maximal intimacy and so maximal vulnerability with and before the people and things sharing our narration.[27]

The emergence of post-cosmopolitan global personhood makes it possible for us to see how systematically the modern was obsessed with boundaries and separation, as well as with the legitimation of its own superiority, and how necessary it is to move beyond this—not to homogenizing collectivism, but to democratic/dialogical relationality in which independence and intimacy are affirmed simultaneously.

Compassion

As oscillation between particular and universal dimensions matures, spiritual practice ripens in the direction of compassion as a more or less sustainable way of life. We develop to the point where we are able to appropriate and, to an ever greater degree, embody what Karen Armstrong identifies as "the lost heart, the spirit of compassion that lies at the core of all of our traditions."[28]

After our initial decision to commit ourselves to a transformative practice, to step across the crucial threshold and consciously engage the work of transformation, we may need to be away from the world for a time, developing in a quiet and protected place. But after a while, a certain urge to "return" begins to appear, an urge that is well articulated in the Zen saying, "Easy to meditate in the monastery, more difficult in the home, most difficult in the world."

As this urge ripens, it begins to morph from the kind of challenge contained in the image of the master cleaning toilets—"meditation" or "enlightenment" right in the midst of the most mundane circumstances—to a more fully engaged love of the world (*Amour Mundi*). It is at this point that we begin to notice and resonate with statements to the effect that wisdom (*prajna*) is identical with compassion (*karuna*). We notice readings of the great traditions that point to 1) incarnation; for example, in Christianity, with simultaneity of the human and the divine and what Dietrich Bonhoeffer calls "religionless Christianity" where "being there for others *is* the experience of transcendence,"[29] 2) return; for example, with the Bodhisattva in Mahayana Buddhism, the "non-returner" who *chooses* to return out of compassion rather than being required to return by her/his *karma* and 3) presence; for example, in the I-Thou relationship, and other fully relational or democratic visions.

INTERPRETATION, CO-CREATIVITY, AND GIFT

We come back to the matter of interpretation with which this essay began and to which it is oriented. The significance of interpretation is well expressed in a statement from William James toward the end of his career: "Philosophies [or interpretations] are intimate parts of the universe, they express something of its own thought of itself. A philosophy may indeed be a most momentous reaction of the universe upon itself."[30] Understanding our interpretations, not just as more or less correct reflections of a single, static orthodoxy, but as intensely personal choices with praxiological and even cosmological implications, is new to Western experience, at least on any widespread basis, and it requires passage through the fire of postmodern relativity and nihilism. It locates humans in a radically different place than that which was assigned by traditional hierarchy and patriarchy. We can now see humans—as in the James' statement—in both passive and active modes. Passively we are media through which the planet transforms itself. Our development, including our interpretations and philosophies, may be our response to what the planet is trying to do. In that case it is not so much that we need to accomplish herculean tasks as to be open to what is already wanting to happen, to stop refusing and let it happen through us, adopting what is perhaps a more Daoist orientation.

Considered actively (and living with the possibility that the most momentous reaction of humans may indeed be *refusal*), humans become co-creators through our choices and what we decide to do with the gift of our lives. We become agents of the ongoing creation of the world, working in concert with the ultimate creative energy, the wellspring of life—however the unnamable comes to be named. The implications in this locational shift could be as momentous as the shift from a geocentric to a heliocentric universe. Tu Weiming speaks of it as the shift from anthropocentrism to an "anthropocosmic" vision[31]

If co-creation—whether through the action of non-action (*wu wei*), or through an active "living to the glory of God"—follows from the above view of interpretation, so also does gift-awareness. Stimulus-response conditioning and chemistry alone do not explain the joy and satisfaction we sometimes feel, the *joie de vivre* that sometimes fills our hearts. And there is no sufficient explanation for the fact that we are *still here,* after the disasters and threats of the past, and in the midst of the ongoing improbabilities of life in the present. There is still no satisfactory answer to Leibniz's question: "Why is there something rather than nothing?" There seems an undeniable quality of gift about our lives, as about the Earth itself floating in the abyss.

This awareness contributes to the same shift we have described with co-creativity. Perhaps most immediately, gift-awareness illuminates the senses in which many (maybe most) of our problems arise from *refusal,* from our attempts to capture, contain, and control the vitality of life rather than accepting its gift quality. It counsels the effort to live more toward gift-responsiveness, rather than toward interactions of exchange or domination.[32] This responsiveness includes not only acceptance of gift but also the *giving* of gift — as the ultimate transformative act or practice — as synonymous with compassion.

This has both personal and political implications of the most momentous sort, including the fact that gift-orientation may be the only posture out of which we will be able to generate the kind of *policy* or institutional adjustments the world so urgently needs for its survival. In fact, it has *cultural* implications as well, offering a persuasive reason for contribution to the common good, beyond the lame myth of the "invisible hand" that legitimated the Western individualism of material self-interest.

In this essay I have offered an interpretation. But above and beyond any advantage this particular interpretation might contain, I recommend we accept the liberation and the responsibility out of which we can recognize the significance of this root function of human life. Our interpretations matter hugely, obviously for those immediately around us and ourselves, and maybe even more broadly in our capacity to decide on the nature of things in more cosmic terms.

This latter realization, while running the risk of anthropocentrism and a generalized overvaluing of the human race, seems to correspond with a sense in which traditional cultures appear to have depended on some persons—the Buddha, Jesus, Mohamed, Confucius, Socrates, Lao Tzu, and others—who were aware of their completely improbable life affirmation in the midst of the great void, some who said "Yes" with full awareness of the absurd and even impossible quality of this act. Now, of course, those "some" who consciously choose must be a much higher proportion of the people than in the traditional past, when we had the energy of those great figures to carry culture for the unconscious masses. With the end of the traditional period in the late 19th century, that source was cut off so that we can no longer be carried. And even more so now, with the collapse of the modern substitution of belief in reason, individuality, and materialism, the carrying capacity of human belief is very weak. .

Perhaps the future depends on those of us who choose the active belief—strange though it may seem—that this *could be* a world of peace, justice, and creative mutuality. Choosing to believe in this way, again, certainly makes a very real difference in our lives and the quality of the lives around us. Who knows, it may also help to heal the planet and move it to a healthier phase.

I return, then, to the assertion with which the essay began: that a new worldview is actually emerging in our midst. It is not "philosophical" in the sense that it can be formulated as a doctrine or package of concepts. Its strongest "argument" is in the way certain people live today, with zest and vision, even in full awareness of the dire and even impossible character of our situation. It is as though they have come to trust an energy that is deeper and more reliable than the all too obvious forces of degradation that populate the surface of our time. But, again, their trust and "believing" is not expressed as intellectual assent, but rather in the quality of what they do and who they are. We should adopt whatever structure of interpretation helps us join them.

ENDNOTES

1. In previous times, this essay might have been identified as soteriology, a description of the process of sanctification or enlightenment; coming from that branch of theology that is concerned with spiritual formation or development. The more appropriate contemporary identification would be with the Chicago School of empirical theology and philosophy of religion, and the Center for Process Studies at Claremont, following Whitehead, Charles Hartshorne, Henry Nelson Wieman, John B. Cobb, Jr., and David Ray Griffin.

2. Alfred North Whitehead, *Adventures of Ideas* (New York: Free Press, 1933), 18.

3. I mention three sources of what I consider to be of real help: the Center for Contemplative Mind in Society (www.acmhe.org/), the Center for Process Studies (www.ctr4process.org/), and the Center for Courage and Renewal (www.couragerenewal.org/).

4. Whitehead, *Adventures of Ideas.*

5. Many today call this orientation "liberalism" or neo-liberalism." I argue that there was in the early modern West another option in which relationships were intrinsically important as the locus of well-being and discovery in the ongoing process of creation. In *Leaving and Returning* I discuss this orientation as "the creating form of association," and in *Overcoming America/America Overcoming*, I use the term "relational liberalism."

6. What I present here is the big picture. See my other work for more detail, especially *Overcoming America/America Overcoming: Can We Survive Modernity?* (Lanham: Rowman and Littlefield, 2012).

7. The kind of contagion and hypnosis I am talking about is well presented in the film, *The Gods Must Be Crazy,* and in Margaret Mead's famous reports of "cargo cults," as the consequence of airplanes flying low over traditional cultures.

8. To cite three helpful sources on this essential point, see Karen Armstrong, *The Great Transformation: The Beginning of Our Religious Traditions* (New York: Alfred A. Knopf, 2006); John Hick, *A Christian Theology of Religions* (Louisville: John Knox Press, 1995); and Jacob Needleman, *The Heart of Philosophy* (New York: Alfred A. Knopf, 1982).

9   Robert N. Bellah, "Religious Evolution," in *Beyond Belief: Essays on Tradition in the Post-Traditional World* (New York: Harper & Row, 1970). This piece remains, for me, one of the most insightful and helpful readings of human history, including the modern and postmodern periods that I am tracking in this essay.

10   Plato, *Phaedo* 114d, in *The Collected Dialogues of Plato,* ed. Edith Hamilton and Huntington Cairns, Bollingen Series, no. 71 (New York: Pantheon Books, 1985), 94; William James, "The Will to Believe," in John J. McDermott, ed., *The Writings of William James* (Chicago: University of Chicago Press, 1977), 731; and Confucius, *Analects* 15:29, in *The Analects of Confucius,* trans. Roger T. Ames and Henry Rosemont (New York: Ballantine, 1998), 190.

11   William Perry, *Forms of Moral and Intellectual Development in the College Years (*New York: Holt, Rinehart and Winston, 1968), 136, 135.

12   This point is utterly crucial and yet very difficult to articulate without sounding like a dizzy romantic. For help in articulation, see the poetry of Gerard Manly Hopkins or Robert Frost (especially "To Earthward"), or Ralph Harper's luminescent *On Presence* (Baltimore: Johns Hopkins University Press, 2006).

13   It is important to be aware that we are not always in a good position to evaluate our practice, so that having a guide or a good friend is almost necessary. The Zen Master Dogen says "the inconceivable may not be distinctly apparent. Its appearance is beyond your knowledge." In Eihei Dogen, *Moon in a Dewdrop: The Writings of the Zen Master Dogen,* ed., Kazuaki Tanahashi (San Francisco: North Point Press, 1985), 15.

14   On this inevitable aspect of practice, one that is closely related to the Dogen point above, see Kierkegaard's *Fear and Trembling* or St. John of the Cross on "the dark night of the soul." Paul Tillich is also very strong on this point, especially in *The Courage to Be.*

15   For practical guidance on beginning contemplative practice, see Thich Nhat Hanh, *The Miracle of Mindfulness* (Boston: Beacon Press, 1977); Jon Kabat-Zinn, *Wherever You Go There You Are* (New York: Hyperion, 1994); and William Johnston, *Christian Zen: A Way of Meditation* (San Francisco: Harper & Row, 1971).

16 What I am saying here is no longer—as it had been throughout most of the modern period—exotic or mysterious, given the relatively recent findings of neuroscience. See, for example, F. Varela, E. Thompson, and E. Rosch, *The Embodied Mind: Cognitive Science and Human Experience* (Cambridge, MA: MIT Press, 1993).

17 Karen J. Warren, *Ecofeminist Philosophy: A Western Perspective on What It Is and Why It Matters* (New York: Rowman and Littlefield, 2000).

18 Amartya Sen, "Democracy and Its Global Roots," in *The New Republic,* 6 October 2003, 35.

19 Sor-hoon Tan "Reconstructing 'Culture:' A Deweyan Response to Antidemocratic Culturalism," in Sor-hoon Tan and John Whalen-Bridge, eds., *Democracy as Culture: Deweyan Pragmatism in a Globalizing World* (Albany: SUNY Press, 2008), 34–35.

20 Several more or less convergent movements of our era carry this basic point, perhaps especially what I refer to as "relational feminism." My best example here is Elizabeth Johnson, *She Who Is* (New York: Crossroad, 1993).

21 Hannah Arendt, *The Human Condition* (Chicago: University of Chicago Press, 1958), 176.

22 Confucius, *Analects* 6.30, 110.

23 John B. Cobb, Jr. *Beyond Dialogue: Toward a Mutual Transformation of Christianity and Buddhism* (Philadelphia: Fortress Press, 1982).

24 Cobb, *Beyond Dialogue,* 52.

25 Masao Abe, "The End of World Religion, in *Zen and Western Thought,* ed., William R. LeFleur (Hololulu: University of Hawaii Press, 1985), 261.

26 See *Overcoming America/America Overcoming,* Chapter 8, 119–20.

27 Peter D. Hershock, *Reinventing the Wheel: A Buddhist Response to the Information Age* (Albany, NY: SUNY Press, 2001), 287.

28 Armstrong, 399.

29 Dietrich Bonhoeffer, *Letters and Papers from Prison* (New York: MacMillan), 381.

30 William James, "A Pluralistic Universe," in *Essays in Radical*

Empiricism and a Pluralistic Universe, ed. Richard J. Bernstein (New York: Dutton, 1971), 272.

31 Tu Weiming, "Beyond the Enlightenment Mentality: A New Perspective on Confucian Humanism," lecture delivered at Grand Valley State University, MI, 5 December 2003.

32 For reflection on this way of thinking about and locating the ultimate, see Calvin O. Schrag, *God Is Otherwise Than Being: Toward a Semantics of the Gift* (Evanston, IL: Northwestern University Press, 2002).

11

TOWARD A RELATIONAL WORLD

From a Western Perspective

WE WANT TO FLIP THE FIGURE-GROUND *GESTALT* of perception to focus on the relation rather than the thing. We want to see in a different way—deeper, broader, with more appreciation and care. We want to stop objectifying, so we will be able to live out of that magic William James called "pure experience," the experience Wittgenstein was talking about when he said, "not *how* the world is, is the mystical, but *that* it is." Or Socrates (then Plato, then Aristotle) when he/they said, "philosophy begins in wonder." Or Adrienne Rich, when she said: "The void is the creatrix, the matrix. It is not mere hollowness and anarchy... The something born of that nothing is the beginning of our truth."[1] We want a new worldview, one that honors these realities, rather than obscuring and denying them.

There is something we are trying to point to. There is something we are trying to say and become, something that stretches us just beyond what we have been at our best, as beings who are capable—despite all kinds of decadence, confusion, and lethargy—of transcending ourselves when we are ready. This is not the something of adolescent religiosity or rebellion, but only what is required if the world and our children are to endure in any but the most miserable of circumstances.

Reaching for an articulation of this "something," as any good philosophy would generally try to do, could provide a resource and support for the process of living into and embodying these best moments. But not in the old mode of articulation as either doctrine or technique, as linear construction of propositional logic or mechanics. We need to speak of and from the origins of our best moments, before they are lost in attempts to capture and contain them in ways that only make them more distant to us. Maybe the most effective articulation comes in the form of what Martin Buber called "pointings," glimpses at a sacred center from several angles of approach, and always remembering with Lao Tzu at the opening of the *Dao De Jing*: "the Dao that can be spoken is not the eternal Dao."[2]

I

Look into the eye of the other and see the Void, that absolute darkness at the center of each eye, that "gateway to the soul" through which the undifferentiated Nothingness becomes most distinctly a living, creating human being, a source of discovery, novelty, and fresh energy in the world. But this is just an eye exam. Now pull focus out from the singular eye to somewhere a few inches in front of the face, where two eyes can be seen simultaneously as the presence of an other. Now we are in the space of the infinitely complex event of an actual encounter, the space where relationality becomes explicit in what Hannah Arendt refers to as "the paradoxical plurality of unique beings,"[3] such that plurality is "the law of the Earth."[4] Now we are in the most sacred open space of the world, the space of Nothingness and possibility in which revelation—and you, and I—might appear when we are together in the mode of compassionate, full presence, and commitment to the common good. Here, in that open space of our being together, we can also make discoveries about matters of mutual interest, solve problems, or — in the dimmer light at the edges of this space — we can negotiate, make deals, compromise, or at least get along with some measure of mutual respect.

Why do we so rarely think or speak of these most basic dynamics? We are so busy in the object world, chasing this, that, or some other, and probably because of the amazingly fragile and highly temporary quality of our existence.

So often we fail to appreciate what is beautiful on this planet (and why it is said that the angels envy us) until it is too late. When you come to me not as dealer or player, function or obligation, but in the mode of relationality, which is to say both most definitely as yourself and at the same time open, free of self-interested agenda or need, you come with no gift other than your presence. You emerge astonishingly and without precedent, out of the vastness, as utterly unique and miraculous. You approach free and yourself, and our meeting might be pure joy. Or we could at least begin the day by greeting each other as sources of this possibility, and then proceed to the shared work and inevitable conflict that arise from loving the world enough to change it.

If we are fortunate and smart, we can accept that the purity of our encounter will not last in this world of distortion and suffering, and have faith that despite this the light still shines, as does the sun on cloudy days through blue sky openings or heavy cloud filter. We keep the relational faith, that primal faith of pure encounter. We are alive, there is goodness to it, and we are not alone.

II

Of course we all emerge from trauma. We are born, paradoxically, both out of nowhere and out of somewhere. And for most of us, a second, distinctly spiritual kind of birth seems to be required by the curriculum of life. Who we are emerges from the relationship with who we have been, and with whom.

Later in the energetic career of William James, he came to see this second birth experience with the kind of understanding I am describing as the source of life's essential vitality. After becoming famous for categorizing the "varieties of religious experience," James concluded his 1909 Hibbert Lectures, later published under the title of *A Pluralistic Universe,* by focusing on a very particular and fundamental kind of experience:

> there *are* religious experiences of a specific nature, not deductible by analogy or psychological reasoning from our other sorts of experience. I think that they point with reasonable probability to the continuity of our consciousness with a wider spiritual environment.[5]

What he is talking about are "experiences of an unexpected life succeeding upon death... the deathlike termination of certain mental processes within the individual's experience, processes that run to failure, and in some individuals, at least, eventuate in despair."[6] He characterizes the unexpected life that follows these moments in terms of "resources in us that naturalism with its literal and legal virtues never wrecks of, possibilities that take our breath away, of another kind of happiness and power, based on giving up our own will and letting something higher work for us."[7] James concludes that "Sincerely to give up one's conceit or hope of being good in one's own right is the only door to the universe's deeper riches."[8]

This theme of an essential relatedness with a deeper self that is paradoxically continuous with "a wider spiritual environment" is echoed far and wide across the world's traditions. The American Christian theologian Paul Tillich speaks of it as experience of "the God who appears when God has disappeared in the anxiety of doubt."[9] The Japanese Kyoto School philosopher Keiji Nishitani says it in a way that, like the feminist Adrienne Rich, cited above, is compelling existentially:

> emptiness is something we are aware of as an absolute near side. It opens up more to the near side than we, in our

ordinary consciousness take our own self to be. It opens up, so to speak, still closer to us than what we ordinarily think of as ourselves. In other words, by turning from what we ordinarily call 'self' to the field of *sunyata*, we become truly ourselves... We take leave of the essential self-attachment that lurks in the essence of self-consciousness and by virtue of which we get caught in our own grasp in trying to grasp ourselves.[10]

These experiences are relational in the depth of encounter with genuine self, and are distinct from being locked up in the striving, ever-anxious, and lonely-isolated objectifying ego. In the paradox of genuineness, they are somehow identical or "continuous" with the creative energy of the cosmos.

It may be a developmental necessity that individuals have at least begun the process of cultivating this fundamental relation between ego and genuine self before they become capable of bearing the creative energy into the world. And surely persons in the world can be transformed through the presence of others in whom the developmental process is well-advanced, such as the Bodhisattva in Buddhism, the enlightened one who returns to the world to help others, or the Judeo-Christian God who "so loved the world" that "his only son" was given for our redemption. In fact, the transformative power of this presence—in more or less intense forms—is at the heart of some interpretations of the traditions arising out of the Axial Age. In Christianity, for example, "where two or more are gathered in my name, there am I in the midst of them" (Matthew 18:20), or "the Kingdom of God is among you" (Luke 17:21), or Dietrich Bonhoeffer's statement that "being there for others is the experience of transcendence."[11] In some religious orientations, the "temple" or "holy place" is not a building, institution, or any kind of geographical space, but relatedness itself as locus of the ultimate. And insofar as movement to capacity for full relatedness is parallel to what social scientists like James Fowler identify as healthy development, developmental thinking can also be seen as pointing toward the relational.¹² Robert Kegan goes so far as to suggest that it may be one of the more optimistic qualities of our time that the very fact of people living longer means that the world has the benefit of contact with the higher levels of human development like never before.¹³

III

All of the above could sound like mystical or romantic babbling, maybe echoes from an enchanted past that is no longer recognized in the mechanized present. Yet if we are to avoid being replaced by the robots who could already be walking among us, there is something deep and ineffable within our nature that needs to be maintained and cultivated, something well and effectively—if incompletely—remembered by priests of solitude like Ralph Harper and Anne Morrow Lindbergh.¹⁴ There is something within us that needs to be honored and deeply attuned to the value of remaining open, as against the temptations of living closed and clouded.

This awareness resonates with my own past in a way that is surprising to me at first, because my discovery is so distinctly not private. In fact, the surprise itself is instructive, since it reveals the tendency to assume that what we need is only to be found in private spaces apart from the world, in the exotic, the "religious," the psychoanalytical, or the wilderness. Again, I do not mean to dismiss the significance of those more private spaces, but only the assumption that they alone—as in the world-denying tendencies of traditional religion—contain what we need in order to thrive.

I had the great good fortune to be among the activists of the American Sixties, one of those who heard Martin Luther King, Jr.'s proclamation in his 1963 "Letter from a Birmingham Jail:" "Now is the time to make real the promise of democracy and transform a pending national elegy into a creative psalm of brotherhood [*sic*]."¹⁵ In my understanding of the story of that time, this was a very palpable call, something heard as compelling and profoundly hopeful by many of my generation. It was as though some possibility from deep under the flow of history had come to the surface, challenging us to respond and promising a kind of sustaining energy if we did.[16]

We did. Across a broad spectrum of issues and causes, people came out. There were self-help centers, civil rights protests, War on Poverty programs, anti-war demonstrations. Race, poverty, and peace provided the issue focus in the early 1960s, in the wake of the monumental 1952 Supreme Court Brown v. the Board of Education ruling that "separate is inherently unequal." But there were also more culturally oriented responses to the call for transformation. The children of Ginsberg and Kerouac's earlier Beatnik generation multiplied in the Sixties into a widespread hippie protest against the shallowness and hypocrisy of middle class life, as the sense of a better possibility began to impact the intergenerational relations of families, schools, and religious institutions.

In the medium of activism, we talked, we deliberated, shared a public life, and enjoyed—without really knowing it at the time—participation in the core meaning of democracy. By today's standards of texting and tweeting, it's amazing how long and intensely we talked. Above and beyond (or under) the issues and alternative actions we were discussing, we were learning the magic of being able to be more fully and authentically ourselves in the presence of others than we could be in private. We were teaching each other the richness we often grasp for today under banners of multiculturalism, diversity, inclusion: a public space not only populated by difference, but where that difference interacts in a specific sort of way to generate energy, beauty, and justice. We were learning democracy first hand, democracy not as structures and mechanism of government, but as what John Dewey called "a mode of associated living, of conjoint, communicated experience"[17] and what global democrats such as Amartya Sen and Sor-hoon Tan refer to as governance by discussion.[18]

I recall reading A. D. Lindsay's magnificent little book, *The Essentials of Democracy* (1929), in the middle of the Sixties and realizing two things. First, strange as it seems in the midst of our astonishing material affluence, few people any more have much sustained and cultivated experience of this most basic human activity. Very different from "chatting," it has to be *about* something, it has to *go* somewhere, and it requires us to be both definite and open in ways that do not come naturally to most of us. And, second, without direct experience of governance by discussion, "democracy" is disconnected from its mooring and adrift, even to the extent of that distinctively modern kind of tyranny de Tocqueville, Nietzsche, and others have identified as "the tyranny of the majority."

It was also at this point that I became aware of the deeply anti-democratic and anti-relational intellectualism of Western culture. When something good (or bad, for that matter) happens, we need to interpret. And the dominant Western way of interpretation became one of abstraction into displaced and static intellectual constructs of "individual" or "community." So when a moment of relationship or democratic life occurred, it was likely interpreted either as individuals combining together in overlapping interests to form a social contract, or some kind of organic or mechanical entity expressing itself through the life of individuals. But not both together in a living reciprocity, not in relationship itself. Relationality needed to be frozen and then understood as either parts determining wholes or wholes determining parts, not the co-presence of both. It's as though the West came to prefer the apparent shelter of intellectual order to the risks of embodied life. Real democracy began to die, or at least failed to receive the cultural/intellectual/artistic support it needs to remain as a real possibility in the world. Perhaps, in the global era, and with the benefit of dialogue with other cultures such as those in Asia that have maintained a healthier affirmation of Nothingness and ineffability, this Western fixation on intellectual order at the expense of the vitality of life is beginning to loosen its grip.

IV

Relationality requires a certain threshold of individual development, as well as a degree of socio-cultural support for activities and experiences of discussion — or what we might more likely today call "dialogue." But engagement with relationality also *generates* this development, such that purely private efforts to cultivate maturity, while possibly producing smart consumers, good negotiators, or even psychologically astute companions, are not likely to inspire citizenship or the art of substantive and reliable friendship. Relationality requires the quality that distinguishes education from training, development from habituation, transformation from information.

Seen in this way, I suggest that much of the creative endeavor of higher education in America today is organized around just such an effort to cultivate the maturity of the relational human being.[19] In these pagers, I have repeatedly referenced the Association of American Colleges and Universities' LEAP programs. These programs are all about the related arts of service learning, civic engagement, diversity, inclusion, and multiculturalism. Of course, these can be understood cynically as faddish distractions from the intellectual and/or occupational purposes of education. They can be viewed in terms of their instrumental value, as media for acquisition of the management skills necessary to success in today's world. But there is something much more to these programs and to the newer emphasis in higher education on "transformative" or "integrative" education by Parker Palmer, Arthur Zajonc, and other leaders in the movement for a new understanding of the purposes and methods of education.[19] One may go so far as to say that these programs are quite literally ushering in the new and distinctly postmodern worldview that is required if we are to survive modernity and its unsustainable habits of materialism and isolation.[20]

Relationality is the heart of the new worldview. It involves the developed capacity of moving beyond 1) traditional absolutism, with one set of right answers and all others in the wrong, and 2) modern relativism, in which any answer is as good (or marketable) as any other. A relational worldview moves us into a pluralism that involves a higher order of hermeneutical sophistication not common in the past. I am speaking of the sophistication to realize that everyone has an interpretation, and all interpretations are limited by the inevitably contingent circumstances out of which they arise. Further, the developed sophistication to which I am pointing sees no reason for adolescent nihilism and/or despair over the complexity of more than one "right answer." It sees no reason to lament the passing of the old culture, with its single, static, detached absolutism, its hierarchy, logocentrism, and patriarchy.

Instead, we can learn an active aesthetic of difference and relationality that is a benefit to ourselves as well as a true service to the other. And more: we find that it is in the presence of the other who is and remains different that we are able to be present from the depth of our genuine self, even in the tumult of ordinary life.

Critics of the transformation-oriented programs in contemporary higher education miss the finer point. Whether the critique is that transformative education is a distraction from 1) the "academic," understood as accumulation of amounts of testable knowledge, or 2) the "professional," understood as acquisition of marketable skills and protocols, the relational worldview understands what the critiques miss: that it is in mutuality that we find ourselves being alive. It is in compassionate presence with the other that we experience fulfillment. It is in the interdependent play of relationality that we are able to walk away from the iron cage of modernity's rationalization of everything for the sake of nothing more than more. Only relationship generates meaning, purpose, and a reliable abode for life on this planet.

ENDNOTES

1   Adrienne Rich, *On Lies, Secrets, and Silence: Selected Prose 1966-1978* (New York: Norton, 1979), 64.

2   Martin Buber, *Pointing the Way,* M. Friedman, ed. (New York: Harper Torchbooks, 1957).

3   Hannah Arendt, *The Human Condition* (Chicago: University of Chicago Press, 1958), 176.

4   Arendt, *Human,* 109.

5   William James, *A Pluralistic Universe,* in *Essays in Radical Empiricism and A Pluralistic Universe,* Richard J. Bernstein, ed. (New York: Dutton, 1971) 264.

6   James, *Pluralistic,* 265.

7   James, *Pluralistic,* 266.

8   James, *Pluralistic.*

9   Paul Tillich, *The Courage to Be* (New Haven: Yale University Press, 1952), 190.

10 Keiji Nishitani, *Religion and Nothingness* (Berkeley: University of California Press, 1982), 151.

11 Dietrich Bonhoeffer, *Letters and Papers from Prison* (New York: MacMillan, 1976,) 381.

12 James Fowler, *Stages of Faith: The Psychology of Human Development and the Quest for Meaning* (San Francisco: Harper & Row, 1981).

13 Robert Kegan, *Over Our Heads: The Mental Demands of Modern Life* (Cambridge: Harvard University Press, 1994).

14 Ralph Harper, *On Presence: Variations and Reflections* (Philadelphia: Trinity Press International, 1991); Anne Morrow Lindbergh, *Gift from the Sea* (New York: Pantheon Books, 1955).

15 Martin Luther King, Jr.'s proclamation in his 1963 "Letter from a Birmingham Jail," in *Why We Can't Wait* (New York: New American Library, 1963), 86.

16 Stephen Rowe, *Leaving and Returning: On America's Contribution to a World Ethic* (London: Associated University Presses, 1989).

17 John Dewey, *Experience and Education* (New York: Macmillan, 1938), 87.

18 Amartya Sen, "Democracy and its Global Roots," *The New Republic,* 6 October 2003, 28–35; and Sor-hoon Tan, *Confucian Democracy:*

A Deweyian Reconstruction (Albany: SUNY Press, 2004).

19 Parker Palmer and Arthur Zajonc, *The Heart and Higher Education: A Call to Renewal* (San Francisco: Jossey-Bass, 2010).

20 In my *Overcoming America/America Overcoming: Can We Survive Modernity?* (Lanham: Rowman and Littlefield, 2012). I present the underlying problematic of modernity, its positive features as well as liabilities, the degree to which there can be "Many Globalizations" (Berger and Huntington), and the worldview of dialogue/relationality/democracy which is emerging through the struggles of our era.

ACKNOWLEDGMENTS

    Much gratitude is owed to Dr. Jeanyne B. Slettom, who is General Editor of the relatively new Process Century Press, and of the Toward Ecological Civilization Series, in which both this book and the conference-related *Educating for an Ecological Civilization* (co-edited with Marcus Ford) appear. Neither of these works could have seen the light of day without Dr. Slettom's amazing combination of publishing skills and practical wisdom.

    I also want to thank Elizabeth M.K. Stemen, a genius of format and copy editing, who appeared quite serendipitously at the time when Marcus and I were nearly drowning in text revisions, copyediting crises, personal requests, and the generalized chaos of publishing an anthology. Just at the right moment Beth showed up, and calmly brought order, competence, and perspective to the project. And she very generously agreed to stay on to work her magic on this project also. She has my undying gratitude.

    Some of the works in this volume have appeared in one form or another in other publications, and I want to acknowledge and thank them:

"Standing Up to Managerialism," in *Liberal Education* 100.3 (Summer 2014).

"Rediscovering Liberal Education in China: On the Benefits of Dialogue and Inquiry," in *Soundings: An Interdisciplinary Journal* 96.2 (Summer 2013).

Overcoming America/America Overcoming: Can We Survive Modernity? (Lanham, MD: Lexington Books, 2012).

"The Adulthood We Need: Education and Developmental Challenge in the U.S. and China," in Judy Whipps, ed., *Reflect, Connect, Engage: Liberal Education at GVSU* (Acton: Xanedu Press, 2013).

"The Other Conversation: Dialogue, Meditation, and Service," in Ford and Rowe, eds., *Educating for Ecological Civilization: Interdisciplinary, Experiential, and Relational Learning* (Anoka, MN: Process Century Press, 2016).

"Pragmatism, Possibility, and Human Development," in *Essays in the Philosophy of Humanism* 23.2 (December 20 15).

"Toward a Relational World from a Western Perspective," in *China Media Research* 11.2 (April 2015).

Finally, I would like to thank my students and colleagues at Grand Valley State University. We are a public, comprehensive, masters large, relatively new effort to engage "liberal education in a public context," and to integrate liberal and career education. Through the ambitiousness—some would say improbability—of our efforts, I have learned enormously, and benefitted from an incredibly rich and informative kind of "field learning" about the senses in which higher education is microcosmic of American culture.

www.ingramcontent.com/pod-product-compliance
Lightning Source LLC
Chambersburg PA
CBHW021144080526
44588CB00008B/215